AMERICAN HOUSES
IN HISTORY

Arnold Nicholson

AMERICAN

HOUSES IN HISTORY

CASTLE BOOKS · NEW YORK

To Elisabeth White Nicholson,
who shares my gratitude to Charles E. Peterson,
architect and historian, for his introduction
to the past that lives and serves us today

First published in 1965 by The Viking Press, Inc.
625 Madison Avenue, New York, N.Y. 10022

Published simultaneously in Canada by
The Macmillan Company of Canada Limited

Library of Congress catalog card number: 65-20157
This edition published by arrangement with THE VIKING PRESS, INC.

CONTENTS

FOREWORD

"Architecture is the most unselfish of the arts, it belongs to passers-by, and every old house and garden . . . is a gift to the nation, to be enjoyed by future generations who will learn from it more history and art and philosophy than may be found in books." — GEORGE SITWELL, *On the Making of Gardens*

The rich and varied heritage of America lives on in houses from its past. Here is history you can see and touch — physical evidence of the people who made our nation. They left clues to their origins, their problems, and their accomplishments in the dwellings that have survived them. At Monticello, for example, Thomas Jefferson reveals his art as an architect and ingenuity as a builder. Generations of Adamses left the mark of their brilliance and accomplishments in the family home at Quincy. The woodworking genius of William Buckland in Virginia and of Samuel McIntire in Massachusetts or the frontier carpentry of French-Canadians in the Mississippi Valley met widely different yet equally significant needs in the early growth of the American dream.

You will meet Spaniards, Swedes, Dutchmen, Frenchmen, Germans, and — most notably — Englishmen in the homes described in this book. The ideas they brought with them to the New World persisted in their dwellings, marking the regions where settlement began. The map on pages 254–255 shows when and where those pioneers traveled and the first homes were built.

This book includes the houses of two and a half centuries, beginning with 1610. Homes built after the Civil War are not included, however, for the continent had been conquered by then, even though much of the West remained yet to be settled. It is divided into geographical segments, beginning with New England, thence down the Atlantic Coast to Florida, the Gulf, up the Mississippi to the Great Lakes, and finally to the Southwest and the

Pacific Coast. A summary of the contents precedes each segment, placing the houses in architectural and historical perspective with each other and with the development of the region.

Architectural quality and significance dictated the choice of most of the houses illustrated, but the people and events associated with them often dominate the text. All of the houses have museum status — that is, they are open to the public, generally for a modest fee, during the season of heaviest travel.

Old Stone House, 1639, Guilford, Connecticut.

Buttolph-Williams House, 1692,
Wethersfield, Connecticut.

Powel House, 1765,
Philadelphia, Pennsylvania.

Monticello, 1775,
near Charlottesville, Virginia.

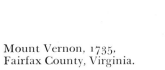

Mount Vernon, 1735,
Fairfax County, Virginia.

Shadows-on-the-Teche, 1831, New Iberia, Louisiana.

I

NEW ENGLAND

1 2 3 P. RE

Boston, 1768.

NEW ENGLAND

When the Pilgrims established their first permanent settlement at Plymouth, Massachusetts, in 1620 they found shelter and security in crude, makeshift structures that were only a memory within a generation. These early dwellings have been reproduced in modern times, but the original huts, the dug-out caves, and the wigwams had a relatively short life. Some of the more substantial homes built by the first generation of settlers, however, have survived.

A stream of immigrants from England — entire families crowded into little ships — flowed steadily to New England. Farming communities and centers of commerce spread. Salem was founded in 1626 and Boston four years later. Farm "towns" were organized from the Merrimac River to Cape Cod. Colonies in Rhode Island, Connecticut, and New Hampshire had similar growth, and nearly all the land within reach of navigable water from Maine's Penobscot River to Connecticut's Naugatuck was thinly populated by 1650.

The families that settled New England came, for the most part, from small villages and farms and brought with them building practices that had persisted in rural England since medieval times. Their new homes, like the old, were built of wood, framed with heavy oak posts and girts, or beams, around a massive central chimney and topped by steeply pitched roofs covered with thatch.

The thatch was soon replaced by more permanent wood shingles, readily obtainable in the forests of the New World. Roofs on the cold north side were extended almost to the ground over a rear shed addition and in time lost the steep pitch that thatch covering had dictated.

Post and girt construction persisted for two centuries — and the houses have proved durable, too. Seventeenth-century wood dwellings survive in surprising numbers from Connecticut to New Hampshire. The oldest — and probably the oldest wood structure in the United

States — is the Fairbanks house at Dedham, just outside Boston. Another early wooden dwelling can be found in the heart of Boston — the house that became Paul Revere's home nearly a century after it was built. It has miraculously survived nearly three centuries of city hazards, including several disastrous fires.

Boston was also one of the few places in New England where masonry houses were erected in the early years. Lime for mortar was hard to come by, except in Rhode Island, and was hoarded for fireplace and chimney construction. Wood was familiar as a building material; it was plentiful and gave good protection against moisture and cold.

The only surviving seventeenth-century stone house in New England is Henry Whitfield's dwelling in Guilford, Connecticut; it was also the fort and meetinghouse for the settlement he founded on Long Island Sound. An approach to masonry construction occurred with the "stone-enders" in Rhode Island, typified by the Arnold house at Lincoln, where the chimney at a gable end was enlarged to form the entire wall.

During the eighteenth century a few New England mansions, such as the Warner house in Portsmouth and the Derby house in Salem, were built of brick in proper English Georgian manner. But wood remained the favorite, often being "rusticated" to imitate masonry block construction, as on the exterior walls of the Wentworth-Gardner house in Portsmouth or at Colonel Jeremiah Lee's Marblehead mansion.

The finest Federal-period homes, built at the beginning of the nineteenth century, are brick. They are found where wealth was concentrated, in such cities as Portland, Salem, Boston, and Providence, and were the work of such men as Charles Bulfinch, Samuel McIntire, and Alexander Parris, who gave a new professional status to architecture.

In the earliest houses, however, the owner was the architect, with assistance from his neighbors who were carpenters and masons. Construction was a communal affair, especially the raising of the heavy oak framing beams. The employment of carpenter-builders and masons developed in villages. They first adapted their designs, born of medieval tradition, to the site and the owner's desires. Later, as Georgian ideas migrated to America at the beginning of the eighteenth century, owners and their carpenter-builders relied on architectural books from Britain.

The British writer-draftsman Batty Langley, self-taught son of a gardener, influenced the appearance of countless homes on both sides of the Atlantic; pediments, cornices, staircases — all the components of the house — followed the designs in his builders' books. American publications appeared in the last half of the eighteenth century and were followed almost exclusively in the nineteenth. Asher Benjamin was the builders' favorite source in these later years.

New England's story, as told in the pages that follow, begins in and around Boston, hub of the universe that Pilgrims and Puritans had established. The architectural record of men and events moves from community to community rather than in time — first to Salem, then to Portsmouth, New Hampshire, and Portland, Maine, then southwest to Rhode Island, and, finally, to Connecticut.

18

There are hundreds of old houses open to the public in the six New England states. Those that are described seemed especially significant for the purposes of this book. A complete list of museums and historic houses, available free from the New England Council, Statler Office Building, Boston, Massachusetts, gives the times when the houses are open, admission charges, and brief descriptions.

Fairbanks Homestead, Dedham, Massachusetts.

Fairbanks
Homestead

Boston's Charles River is nearly as unpredictable in its meanderings en route to Back Bay as the streets in the city itself. Tracing its course upstream takes you for a time roughly parallel to looping Route 128, far south of the metropolis, until the little stream suddenly bends west toward its headwaters.

The town of Dedham is located at this point astride what is now highway U. S. 1, the road to Providence and cities down along the Atlantic coast. In 1793 it was made part of the first national highway in the United States, reaching from Portsmouth, New Hampshire, to Williamsburg, Virginia. Originally it was an Indian trail.

This was the inland spot where a venturesome band of Puritans established a farming community in 1636. One of them was Jonathan Fayerbanke, who had brought his wife and six children to New England from Yorkshire, England, three years earlier. He built his house on a little knoll at the edge of a brook that flowed into the Charles, establishing a home that was lived in by his descendants for two hundred and seventy years and is still a Fairbanks property, maintained as a museum by the family.

Jonathan's homestead, with the additions he made in 1648 and 1654, is America's most remarkable survival from the period of English settlement in the early years of the seventeenth century. It is the oldest wood-frame structure in the United States. Moreover, it has never been extensively rebuilt to restore it as a "period piece." The eight generations of Fairbankses who occupied the house made their share of improvements but in the long process preserved, both inside and out, the architectural integrity of their inheritance from Jonathan. The most conspicuous change occurred in the windows, all of which date from the eighteenth century or later, but the family possessions displayed indoors include a number of the small diamond-pane casement sashes that Jonathan undoubtedly installed after building his house.

The central, 1636–1637 portion of the house is the typical two-room-on-each-floor, central

Jonathan Fayerbanke built his home in 1636 in Dedham, outside Boston. It is probably the oldest wood structure in the United States and a good example of the Colonial house that grew with its family. The north side is mostly roof, for weather protection. The gable-

roofed addition with the chimney, facing the street, was built in 1648; the other in 1654. The brick fireplace and oven were built into the huge original fireplace in the eighteenth century. The house has been owned by the family for over three hundred years.

chimney design brought from medieval England. The front of the house faces south to take advantage of winter sunlight, while the north is almost entirely roof, with the steep pitch of the main part breaking into the shallower slope of a shed which extends almost to the ground. The north-side lean-to, which provided storage space and was often converted to kitchen use, was the the settlers' answer to the cold, stormy winters they encountered in New England.

The gabled-roofed addition to the east, next to the highway, was built in 1648, presumably for Jonathan's oldest son, John, and his bride. It has two rooms below, heated by corner fireplaces which share the same chimney, its own stairs, and a single room on the second floor. Another gable-roofed addition, without a chimney, was added to the west of the main house in 1654. An odd little "porch" or entranceway, with a ceiling that looks like an inverted wooden tray, gives access to the 1648 addition from outdoors.

The doorway to the main part of the house opens into its own "porch," which we would call a hall today. This tiny space contains the stairs, which wind to the floor above, and gives access to the rooms on each side through doors. The all-purpose room to the left was known as the "hall," while the "parlor" was on the right. The hall was the family room and kitchen combined, in some locations known as the keeping room. The huge cooking fireplace in the Fairbanks homestead was partially bricked in when an oven and other eighteenth-century improvements were added. The west wall of the Fairbanks hall, however, is covered with an overlapped, beaded board wainscotting believed to be the original interior finish.

Fayerbanke, like other early New Englanders, believed in insulation. The space between exterior and interior wood walls in early homes usually was filled with a variety of nogging — seaweed; soft, unburned brick; or clay-daubed wattle. Bricks are visible behind an interior board removed from the north wall of the Fairbanks homestead hall, and clay-covered sticks, arranged like lath, can be seen in the room above.

The furniture, utensils, and other objects within the house are all associated with the Fairbanks family and make up a delightfully intimate commentary on home life in America through three centuries. The Fairbanks Family Association has maintained the homestead since 1903. It is open from May 1 until November 1, every day except Monday.

The Adams
"Old House"

The rambling, gambrel-roofed structure in Quincy, Massachusetts, that housed two Presidents is best known today as the Adams mansion. The Adamses themselves, typically, had less pretentious ideas about the home that four generations of the family had known, from 1788 to 1927. It was simply and affectionately called the "Old House," where the tangible evidence of their busy, influential lives accumulated in room after room.

When John and Abigail Adams returned from Great Britain in 1788 and moved into the house she called it a "wren's nest." The structure then was less than half its present size — just two rooms with a stair hall between on both the first and second floors, topped by a dormered attic. This is the west half of the front section of the house and was built in 1730–1731.

John had purchased it, while they were still abroad, from the heirs of the builder Major Leonard Vassall, a wealthy sugar planter who had come to Massachusetts from the West Indies in 1727. He had a town house in Boston and bought farm land in the community then known as Braintree. He obviously did not rely entirely on country carpenters to build his country home, for the elegant and unusual mahogany paneling that survives in the parlor and the finely detailed west staircase suggests skills brought from Boston, only eight miles away.

John and Abigail apparently joined the separate rear kitchen to the house after they moved in. In 1800, the final year of his term as President, they doubled the size of their home by adding a second entry hall and staircase and the "Long Room" wing to the east. The second-floor room above became the former President's study — a place for the books and correspondence that occupied him when he was not busy with the "Old House" farm or his substantial holdings of real estate. He died in 1826, the year after his son, John Quincy Adams, was elected sixth President. The comfortable wing chair in which he liked to read and in which he died remains in a bright corner of the room.

Abigail Adams.

John Adams.

The Adams mansion — or "Old House," as the Adams family called it — was built in Quincy, Massachusetts, by Major Leonard Vassall in 1730–1731. From 1788 to 1927 four generations of the family lived there — among them two Presidents.

The Long Room contains Abigail's white-painted chairs and several Victorian pieces, along with portraits of John and Abigail, of John Quincy and Charles Francis; all celebrated golden wedding anniversaries here.

It was John Quincy Adams who added the long passage along the north side of the house to connect the two ells, or wings, and the rooms and hallways in between. This was in 1836, during his long and unprecedented service as a member of Congress after he had served a term as President. John Quincy Adams and his son, Charles Francis, used the "Old House" principally as a summer home. Like John, however, they brought to the house the portraits, the furniture, and the other prized family possessions it now holds.

The Long Room is the most interesting for its associations. Portraits of John and his Abigail, of John Quincy and Charles Francis keep watch in this room, where all celebrated golden wedding anniversaries. Abigail's white-painted chairs and sofa, her reminder of early years abroad, still dominate the furnishings, which include pieces in many styles, through the Victorian era. The French doors on either side of the Long Room fireplace were an 1850 change, replacing windows and opening to a piazza that has since been removed.

This alteration to the east gable echoed the work of John and Abigail two generations earlier, when they cut windows through Major Vassall's solid brick west gable to let more light into the rooms on the first and second floors. An interesting relic of the Vassall period is the half-width window in the second-story front, which gave light to a closet at that point. A similar window on the first floor below was closed when the west windows were installed.

Charles Francis Adams made the last addition to the house, enlarging the kitchen and service wing on the west in 1869. Shortly thereafter he built the stone library that overlooks the garden his grandmother Abigail found and perpetuated. The dwarf boxwood that lines the paths is said to have been planted by the Vassalls, and Abigail in her diary speaks of the "Yorkist" rose which still grows in her garden.

Brooks Adams, the youngest of Charles Francis's four sons, was the last of the family to occupy the "Old House." It was his love for the place, reinforced by the memories his brothers Henry and Charles Francis the younger wove into their books, that led to the formation by the family of the Adams Memorial Society shortly after his death in 1927. The Society maintained the house as a museum open to the public during summer months until 1946, when it was deeded to the United States and became a National Historic Site under the care of the National Park Service. It is open each year from mid-April till early in November.

"Old House" is not preserved as a period piece. Like the White House, its environment introduces visitors to many periods of our nation's history. The story is told through the eyes of only one family, but the perspective is exciting, for the members of that family almost always played important roles in crucial events, and the final chapter was written at "Old House" only a generation ago.

Boston and Bulfinch:

Harrison Gray Otis
House

Boston is one of the fortunate cities with an architectural heritage that seems secure. Expressways and monolithic structures may destroy the old profile around its congested perimeter, but Beacon Hill remains. The gold dome of the State House is an apex for the business community, the tenements, the homes of the wealthy, and the grassy slopes of Boston's Common.

Charles Bulfinch was the architect who designed the State House and created the environment on Beacon Hill. His Boston is the city of one hundred and sixty years ago. The heritage of earlier years must be sought in the crooked streets down the north slope, toward the harbor. The home of Paul Revere in North Square, restored to its original external appearance shortly after the fire of 1679, is the only survivor, in that waterfront area, of the city's first half century.

It is the west side of Beacon Hill that cherishes the architectural heritage of Bulfinch and his followers. The period of construction was Federal — the last years of the eighteenth century and the first of the nineteenth. The young nation was safely past its infancy and in its time of greatest growth. War abroad was America's opportunity for trade on the high seas. Boston, in particular, prospered and grew. Fortunes were made almost overnight.

One of the young men who became wealthy was Harrison Gray Otis, a lawyer and a leader in Federalist politics. He turned to Bulfinch for the design of a mansion in 1796. Otis was not yet thirty. Bulfinch had returned from a grand tour of Europe six years earlier, captivated by the light and spacious mood of the new classical movement, especially as it was interpreted by the Scotsman, Robert Adam, and his brothers. The Boston architect's new houses, larger, brighter, more refined and sophisticated than those of Colonial times, became a Boston symbol of wealth and good taste.

Bulfinch designed three houses for Otis on the slopes of Beacon Hill in a period of twelve years. Those at 85 Mount Vernon Street and 45 Beacon Street are on the favored far west.

The Harrison Gray Otis house was designed and built in 1796 by Charles Bulfinch in the spacious and sophisticated mood of the neoclassical movement, which he had observed in Europe.

Mrs. Harrison Gray Otis.

The elegant dining room, with its exquisitely decorated mantel and Adamesque ornaments, helped make the first house of the future United States senator and mayor of Boston a symbol of that city's wealth and good taste.

The first house, however, the finest of them all, is to the northwest, at 141 Cambridge Street. This brick mansion was completed and occupied by Otis in 1797. It is the headquarters and museum today for the venerable Society for the Preservation of New England Antiquities, an organization that maintains forty-five houses of historic and architectural interest from Maine to Connecticut.

The magnificent interior Bulfinch created for Otis was almost intact when the house was acquired by the society in 1916, although the front façade was half-hidden by a row of stores along Cambridge Street, and both the semicircular porch at the front entrance and the Palladian window above it had disappeared. The Society in time not only got rid of the shops and restored the original façade but also moved the entire structure forty feet when Cambridge Street was widened twenty years ago.

Otis and his young wife Sally, the daughter of William Foster, had their drawing room on the second floor. This was, and remains, a salon of superb proportions and elegance. Between the chastely scaled dado and finely detailed cornice, the Adamesque friezes on the mantel and on the entablatures above the doors are focal points that accent the classic grace of the room — a perfect setting for the white-stocked Otis, who, in John Quincy Adams's opinion, excelled any man he knew in entertaining friends.

The dining room, on the first floor directly below the drawing room, opened at the rear to a serving pantry. The kitchen was located in an ell beyond. Both of these rooms for entertaining are located in the west half of the house, which has a wide center hall, handsomely lighted by its Palladian windows on the landing at the rear and on the second floor above the entrance porch. There are two rooms — a parlor and a study — to the east of the hall on the first floor, with two bedrooms above. There are four bedrooms on the third floor.

The principal rooms are decorated and furnished by the society much as the Otises must have maintained the mansion during the five years it was their home. The year he retired from Congress they moved to Mount Vernon Street, setting the pace for the development of that part of Beacon Hill with a new and larger house designed by Bulfinch. Their taste in architecture remains fashionable and a symbol of Boston to this day.

House of the
Seven Gables

You are never very far from the harbor in Salem, Massachusetts, and the houses that take you back to the seaport beginnings of the city are right at the water's edge. Captain John Turner's dwelling, better known as the House of the Seven Gables, was built facing south across the harbor in 1668, when the Puritan settlement was only forty-two years old.

The Turner residence at first had only four gables — at the east and west ends of the house, and two so-called Gothic gables projecting toward the south. The wind-swept north side of this original house became one great expanse of roof, a sweeping S almost to the ground, when a kitchen lean-to was added. There was one massive central chimney. The present picturesque building, with seven gables in all, resulted when Turner added the big gabled wing to the south in 1678 and at the same time built the small gabled "porch" or entranceway in the ell between the new addition and the original building.

The captain's son, John Turner II, made several outstanding changes in the house. He is believed to have put the secret stairs in the huge central chimney for the protection of his sisters when Salem's notorious witch hangings occurred in 1692; a kitchen chimney had been added to the north side of the house, making the old flue available. Thirty years later he paneled and decorated the south wing in "modern" Georgian fashion. The double-sash windows now in the house, also a Georgian improvement, probably replaced smaller seventeenth-century casement windows at that time.

Nathaniel Hawthorne, who was a frequent visitor in the house when it was occupied by his cousin, Susan Ingersoll, gave the house its present name through his novel, *The House of the Seven Gables*, published in 1851. Although Hawthorne never confirmed that Turner's old residence was the setting for his fiction, the association was obvious enough to give the house the fame it deserved. It was rescued from neglect more than half a century ago by Miss Caroline O. Emmerton and carefully restored and has long served a dual life as a mecca for tourists and a neighborhood settlement house. The house is open all year.

Nathaniel Hawthorne, one of the few men permitted to call by Susan Ingersoll, his spinster cousin, wrote the novel *The House of the Seven Gables*, which gave the house its rightful fame.

Captain John Turner built the House of the Seven Gables in Salem, Massachusetts, in 1668. The picturesque house with its almost Elizabethan character lived and changed with its people. It grew from two rooms to fourteen, once had as many as eight gables, and hid a secret staircase in a chimney through which the Turner women could escape the Salem witch-hunts. The parlor is finished in the Georgian manner. The portrait of Captain Turner is by John Smibert.

The House of Seven Gables

Elias Haskett Derby is said to have become America's first millionaire when he and his father opened new trade routes to the Orient with their fleet of ships.

In 1761, Captain Richard Derby, as a wedding present to his son, constructed the typically symmetrical Georgian mansion with its pedimented doorway, gabled roof, and towering pairs of chimneys. Its excellent craftsmanship and taste are especially apparent in the interior.

The Essence of Salem:

Derby Mansion
&
Pingree House

In 1761 Captain Richard Derby began construction of a brick mansion two blocks west of the famous House of the Seven Gables, within sight of the long stone wharf he built about the same time. He had the house built as a wedding present to his son, Elias Haskett Derby, said to have been America's first millionaire — thanks to the fleet ships he and his father sent out from Salem. The Derbys fitted out eighty-five privateers during the Revolution, and Elias Haskett's ships opened new trade routes to the Orient. This was a great, and fabulously profitable, leap from the West Indies and the Mediterranean, where Salem had traded for a century or more.

The house is the oldest brick dwelling in Salem — a typically symmetrical Georgian mansion, with a pedimented doorway, gambrel roof, and towering paired chimneys in the end walls. The paneled rooms have been restored to their original paint colors. The gray-blues and greens typical of the eighteenth century are a strong contrast to the chaste, classical white woodwork found in Salem's predominantly Federal-period houses. The staircase in the center hall is notable for the ornate carving of the balusters.

Salem's old Custom House, just up the street at the head of Derby Wharf, is a sample of Federal design, as is the Hawkes house next door, which was completed in 1801 by Benjamin Hawkes after Samuel McIntire's design. The Wharf, Custom House, and Derby Mansion are all maintained by the National Park Service as part of Salem Maritime National Historical Site. Exhibits in the Custom House explain the history of the port. Objects associated with Nathaniel Hawthorne, including his desk, are also displayed; Hawthorne worked in the building as surveyor of the port from 1846 to 1849, at the time he was gathering material for his novel, *The Scarlet Letter*.

The Derby house is open every day of the year except Thanksgiving, Christmas, and New Year's Day.

The architect who left his mark on Salem was neither a witch-hunter nor a millionaire but the wood-carver and master builder named Samuel McIntire. He was the craftsman who designed and built the finest mansions at a time when Salem's wealth was at its peak — the period extending from just after the Revolution into the early years of the nineteenth century, when Salem's swift sailing ships traded with the world. The large handsome houses that ring Salem's Common and dignify Essex, Chestnut, and Federal Streets were not all McIntire's work; only a few qualify, but many reflect the influence he exerted as the local master of design and ornamentation in the style we call Federal today.

McIntire's finest work can be seen at Pingree House on Essex Street, the scene of a much-publicized murder 134 years ago. This mansion, named for the family that occupied it for generations, had been owned by a Captain Joseph White before it came to the Pingrees. While asleep in his second-floor bedroom, Captain White was bludgeoned and stabbed to death by persons who remained unknown for more than a month. The long search for the culprit, which touched one of Salem's most prominent families, was exploited day after day in the press. Finally, a respected young sea-captain who had married Captain White's grand-niece confessed that he had helped his brother commit the crime. The newspapers had a final field day when the famed Daniel Webster was brought to Salem by the White family to lend his eloquence to the prosecution of the murderers. But there are no relics of this crime in the house today. It is filled, instead, with furnishings that match the Adamesque elegance McIntire achieved in the building itself. Some of the pieces assembled by the Essex Institute, which maintains the house, have been attributed to McIntire — notably a sofa and chairs in the front parlor.

The Pingree house, built in 1804, shows how McIntire refined the "new design" he had learned from Boston's Charles Bulfinch about ten years earlier. The brick house proclaims its heritage in its semicircular portico supported by four slender Corinthian pillars. The doorway is framed by reeded pilasters and side lights, with an elliptical fanlight above. The interior woodwork fulfills the promise of the graceful entranceway; delicate roping and pearling relieve flat wood surfaces, with carved grapes, horns of plenty, and McIntire's familiar baskets of fruit and sheaves of wheat used for accents at strategic points.

McIntire recorded his first impressions of the new style in the sketch pad he took to Boston; a number of the drawings are preserved among his papers. The Peirce-Nichols house on Federal Street contains a delightful, fully realized contrast between his early, Georgian woodwork and his refined, delicate Federal design. The west parlor of this house is elaborately paneled in the fashion popular in 1872, when McIntire built it for the shipping merchant Jerathmiel Peirce. In 1801 Peirce had the larger east parlor done over in McIntire's new style to celebrate the wedding of his daughter, Sally, to George Nichols. Like Pingree House, the Peirce-Nichols house is maintained by the Essex Institute.

The first owner of the Pingree mansion was, of course, a captain — Captain John Gardiner. Both he and Captain White were members of the famous East India Marine Society, a benevolent social organization that proclaimed the source of its members' wealth in trade

38

Pingree House in Salem was built for John Gardiner in 1804. It was designed by Samuel McIntire, the builder and wood-carver who mastered the style we call Federal today, and possesses an atmosphere of restrained opulence characteristic of old Salem. The interiors match the subtle refinements of McIntire's Adamesque elegance.

with the Orient. Today, the hall of the Society on Essex Street is the Peabody Museum, where ships' figureheads, scrimshaw, and objects brought from the corners of the earth by Salem's mariners are on display.

McIntire's death in 1811 at age fifty-four almost coincided with the end of Salem's great prosperity. Ships, the source of Salem's wealth for almost two hundred years, had brought riches that, at their peak, found expression in McIntire's work for future generations to enjoy. The embargoes of war years were followed by the era of the clipper ships, too large for Salem's shallow harbor. Thrifty New Englanders later turned from the sea to manufacturing in search of profits.

The Pingree House is open Tuesday through Thursday all year and also Sunday, June through September; the Peirce-Nichols house is open Tuesday through Saturday all year.

From Fortress to Barony:

Garrison House
&
Lady Pepperell Mansion

Two dwellings within a few miles of Portsmouth, New Hampshire, exemplify in striking fashion the conflict and conquest that accompanied the settlement of New England. The Garrison House in Exeter, New Hampshire, is a relic of the seventeenth-century defenses against the Indian tribes, whereas the Lady Pepperell mansion at Kittery, Maine, celebrates the British-American victory at Louisburg, Nova Scotia, in 1745, which blocked France from the Atlantic Coast.

The Garrison House on Water Street in Exeter was built about 1650 by John Gilman, councilor to the royal governor Edward Cranfield and prominent in the little settlement at the falls of the Exeter River, where he had erected two mills. Gilman's home was a privately owned fortress serving the community; the walls were constructed of heavy, squared logs instead of the thin boards customarily used to sheathe a dwelling. Garrison houses, however, were not log cabins built of rounded, peeled logs. Their hewn timber walls, six inches thick and usually oak, were dovetailed at the corners. They replaced girts, but in other respects the garrison was framed in the manner the colonists had brought from England.

Garrison houses were erected in almost every community remote from such fortified centers as Portsmouth. Only a few survive, and their original construction is usually concealed by later additions to the building and by clapboards applied to the old log walls. Exeter's Garrison House also lost its fortress appearance. It became the nucleus of the town's most prominent mansion when General Peter Gilman, grandson of the builder, added a Georgian wing in 1702. The wainscotted and paneled elegance in this addition is a sharp contrast to the scratch-molded beams that were the only attempt to ornament the early garrison.

The present owner of the house, however, has removed a portion of the addition so that the construction of the original can be viewed from the stone foundation to the roof. The

The Garrison house in Exeter, New Hampshire, was built about 1650 by John Gilman. It served as his home and as a community fortress against Indian raids. Clapboards were later applied to the façade of the house to conceal the original log walls.

The thick walls and small window are typical. The slit in the puncheon floor of this upstairs room was cut along the overhang so that attackers below could be fired upon.

Sir William Pepperell — oil painting by John Smibert.

Lady Pepperell, who insisted upon the use of her title even after the Revolution, built her house in 1760 in Kittery, Maine, as a monument to Sir William Pepperell; she died thirty years after him. Sir William, a soldier-merchant, received the only American baronetcy for leading his regiment to victory at Louisburg in 1745. The aristocratic Georgian dignity of the exterior of the house is equally well expressed inside.

1650 house was rectangular in shape, with an overhanging second story. Slit openings were cut in the puncheon floor along the overhang so that the attackers below could be fired upon. The small windows in the house were hardly more than loopholes. Gilman's medieval fortress home was equipped with a portcullis behind the hinged front door. The heavy planks that were lowered to resist access, even with a battering ram, no longer exist. But the wooden pulley from which they were suspended can still be seen. It was set into the massive oak summer beam which helps frame the structure above the entranceway.

The house left the Gilman family when Peter, who had no heirs, died in 1788. It was bought by a Yankee inventor, Ebenezer Clifford, best known for a diving bell he successfully tested in Portsmouth harbor.

Portsmouth harbor, at the mouth of the Piscataqua River, is the dividing point between New Hampshire and Maine. The Maine side of the harbor is bordered by Kittery Point, and here, in 1760, the widow of Sir William Pepperell built her home as a monument to her distinguished husband, and to the title and the fortune he had left her.

The home of Lady Pepperell, who survived her husband by thirty years, is quite as aristocratic in its Georgian dignity as the manor houses of the Tidewater South, but built of wood instead of brick. It is not a large house, but its pedimented bay, rusticated quoins at the corners, and end chimneys towering above the hip roof are impressive in combination, and obviously designed to fit the station of Lady Pepperell, née Mary Hirst of Boston, whose husband was the first and only American-born baronet and the owner of much of the land that lay along the coast between the Piscataqua and Saco Rivers.

Pepperell's fortune and fame were derived from his victory over the French garrison at Louisburg. He had raised and financed the regiment which made the assault. George II summoned him to London to bestow his title, and Sir William's subsequent business ventures were estimated to have brought him, at the time of his death in 1759, more than a quarter of a million pounds.

The Lady Pepperell house, which is owned by the Society for the Preservation of New England Antiquities, is furnished throughout with fine period antiques. A few personal possessions of the Pepperells are displayed, notably Sir William's handsomely figured silk waistcoat and his lady's patchbox and brocaded slippers. The house is open from mid-June to mid-September. The Garrison House can be seen from May to October 15.

Portsmouth's Wentworths:

Warner House

New Hampshire's toehold on the Atlantic — a fifteen-mile strip sandwiched between Massachusetts and Maine — was established by a settlement at the mouth of the Piscataqua River in 1623. The settlers, who had spent two months on their voyage across the Atlantic, feasted on the wild strawberries at the river's edge and called their new home Strawbery Banke. Twenty years later they renamed it Portsmouth to honor their founder, Captain John Mason, a native of Portsmouth, England. Portsmouth was the capital of New Hampshire throughout the Colonial period, and Strawbery Banke was all but forgotten until the city recently returned the name to a portion of the old town now being restored to its eighteenth-century appearance. Mason, too, took a back seat. Wentworth became the name to conjure with in Portsmouth before the town was a century old.

Three generations of Wentworths governed New Hampshire and left their architectural mark on Portsmouth. The most interesting of the surviving mansions linked to the family is known as the Warner house. In the heart of modern Portsmouth, only a block from the bridge across the river to Kittery, Maine, it was erected shortly after 1716, the year in which Lieutenant Governor John Wentworth's daughter Sarah married Captain Archibald Macphaedris; she is said to have received the land as a dowry. The canny and wealthy Macphaedris had come from Scotland to trade and ship furs and later was best known as the proprietor of an iron works a few miles inland from Portsmouth. Warner House got its name from Jonathan Warner, who married Macphaedris's daughter, Mary. Warners and their collateral descendants lived in it for two centuries.

This mansion was probably the finest in town and is one of the earliest and handsomest Georgian brick dwellings in New England. It is topped by a gambrel roof which supports a six-sided cupola, or observation tower, and is surrounded by a balustrade. This look-out over the waterfront was not part of the original structure, however. The first roof apparently consisted of two gables, with a deep valley extending the length of the house between

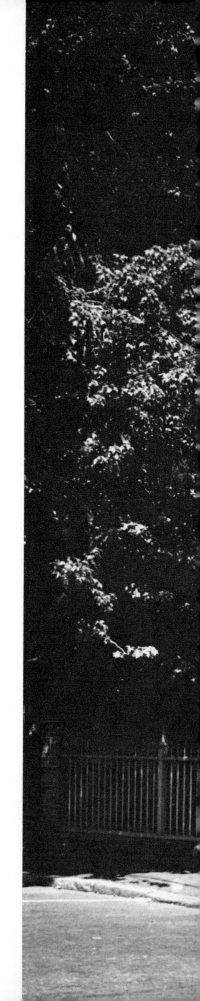

Shortly after 1716 Captain Archibald Macphaedris built Warner House in Portsmouth. The dignified three-story brick dwelling, Georgian in style, was elaborate and costly for its time. The gabled roof is topped with a lightning rod erected in 1762 — probably the first installation of Benjamin Franklin's invention in New Hampshire — and an observation tower for watching the waterfront. The primitive mural paintings on the walls of the stairs landing represent Indian chiefs who were presented at the court of Queen Anne in 1710.

Jonathan Warner, trader, merchant, citizen, lived through and influenced his community and country during the critical years of the American Revolution, the early Republic, and the War of 1812. The painting is by Joseph Blackburn.

them. Such construction was often employed for houses of more than usual depth in medieval England, but it was a poor idea in the New World, where heavy snow accumulated, as Macphaedris soon must have discovered. Lightning, like snow, is more severe in the New World, and the Warners in 1762 equipped their home with a rod believed to have been the first erected in New Hampshire. Benjamin Franklin is said to have supervised this installation of the device he had invented a decade earlier.

The walls of the center hall are decorated with primitive mural painting. Two Indians flank the arched window on the stairs landing. They represent two chiefs who, among others, were presented at the court of Queen Anne in 1710. A scene in the lower part of the hall depicts the taking of the fort at Louisburg, Nova Scotia, by Sir William Pepperell, when France's ambitions in New England were thwarted for all time.

The mansion was purchased by the Warner House Association in 1931. Some family furniture and portraits of members of the Warner family painted by Joseph Blackburn in 1761 were acquired. Pieces on loan from museums and individuals complete the paneled rooms much as Jonathan and Mary Warner must have furnished them.

The earliest of the Wentworth establishments, known today as the Wentworth-Coolidge mansion, belonged to Benning Wentworth, the first royal governor appointed by George II when New Hampshire became a separate province in 1741. The house was begun in 1690 as a farm home and is located on the shore of Little Harbor, southeast of the city. Many additions were made to keep pace with the ambitions of the high-living royal governor, who shocked the community by marrying his pretty young housekeeper after his wife's death. The house was given to the State of New Hampshire a decade ago by Mrs. J. Templeman Coolidge, of Boston.

The mother of the last of the royal governors, John Wentworth, had the Wentworth-Gardner house built in 1760 as a gift to John's younger brother, Thomas. It was built at the water's edge, facing the river. The house was later owned by Major William Gardner.

The structure is wood, with a rusticated block façade and quoins at the corners to give the appearance of stone construction — a treatment frequently used by Georgian designers in New England. The interior woodwork is especially fine, the work of skilled carpenters and joiners which is said to have required fourteen months to complete. The Metropolitan Museum of Art at one time owned the house and proposed to move it to Central Park, in New York. It is now maintained by the Wentworth-Gardner and Tobias Lear Houses Association and open during the summer.

The Warner house is open daily from early May through October.

Down East Elegance:

Tate House,
Sweat Mansion,
&
Victoria Mansion

Maine has always been frontier country, with her fortunes tied to endless evergreen forests and to the sea. The first century and a half of settlement in this vast northern province of Massachusetts was a time of peril from the Indians and the French. The tough, taciturn Down Easters, who did not establish their own state until 1820, were too busy with survival to build mansions in the early years.

The hazards of life in outpost Maine were renewed when the Revolution began. In 1775 the British dispatched a small naval force to Casco Bay and destroyed the principal town, Falmouth, which was rebuilt and incorporated in 1786 as Portland. Only a handful of notable houses built before the Revolution survive. One is in Portland and escaped the torch of the British because it was outside the old town of Falmouth and had been built by George Tate, mast agent for the British navy, whose job was to secure the tallest, soundest trees; each tree over a certain circumference was marked with an arrowhead to indicate that it belonged to the king.

The Tate house dates from 1755. It is a two-and-a-half-story residence with an unusual gambrel roof, recessed at the break in its pitch for a bank of windows in the attic rooms. The principal chambers are handsomely paneled in the Georgian manner. The house is maintained by the National Society of Colonial Dames in Maine and open during the summer, except Mondays.

Sea-faring Maine prospered as long as ships were built of wood, in many years launching more hulls than all other states put together. Portland, until 1832, was the state's first capital. Much of the city was again destroyed by fire in 1866. Fortunately, some of the finest residences built during the period between 1785 and the Civil War are to be found in the area that escaped the flames.

The surviving houses include the first brick dwelling in Portland, built in 1785. It was the childhood home of Henry Wadsworth Longfellow and is maintained as a Long-

The Tate house (*above*) was built by George Tate in 1755 in Falmouth, now Portland. The two-and-a-half-story residence with its unusual gabled roof has a handsome Georgian paneled interior, partly shown in a view of the staircase (*above left*).

In 1800 Alexander Parris designed the Leonardo da Vince Sweat mansion (*far left*) for Hugh McClellan, the first owner. The fine Federal dwelling was bought by Colonel Sweat in 1880. The superb central hall (*left*), shown with its staircase, has a semicircular entrance portal with a Palladian window above.

Henry Austin, the undisputed master of the eclectic, designed Victoria Mansion. It was built from 1859 to 1863 for Ruggles Sylvester Morse and his wife. A combination of many past architectural styles can be seen in the large brownstone house, which is topped by a bell-tower. The interior (*above right*) is lavishly decorated.

fellow museum by the Portland Historical Society, which has its offices in an adjoining building on Congress Street. Only a few blocks away, on High Street, the Portland Society of Art has in its charge the city's finest Federal dwelling, the Leonardo da Vinci Sweat mansion. The house was built in 1800 for Hugh McClellan, a wealthy merchant; his architect was Alexander Parris, a Boston designer who worked with Bulfinch. McClellan lost his fortune and the property in 1814 because of the shipping embargoes associated with the War of 1812. Charles Clapp, son of the wealthiest man in New England, bought the mansion in 1820, and his heirs sold it to Colonel Sweat in 1880.

Colonel Sweat's widow left the house and an endowment to the Society of Art in 1908. Retention of the late Victorian furnishings and alterations in the mansion was her wish; and it is only within recent years that the Society obtained permission to restore the house to its original condition and to furnish the rooms with graceful pieces from the Federal period.

The ornate and grandiose environment of Victorian times, however, has a shrine in Portland, maintained by a female organization dedicated to preserving "the cultural, historical and moral advances made during the reign of Queen Victoria in England." Victoria Mansion, which the Victoria Society of Maine Women opens to visitors every summer, is a monumental example of the style wealth commanded on the eve of the Civil War.

The house, begun in 1859 and completed in 1863, was designed by Henry Austin for Ruggles Sylvester Morse and his wife. Austin was the undisputed master of the eclectic, combining many architectural styles of the past. Greek, Roman, Gothic, Tuscan, French, and Moorish influences are all visible in the big brownstone dwelling topped with a belltower, or campanile. Here is "high" Victorian, the conclusion of designers' enthusiasm for classic forms, which began with the return to "pure," and graceful, Greek and Roman ideas at the beginning of the nineteenth century.

The interior of the house is lavishly decorated. The towering center hall, open to the third floor, has a flying staircase of San Domingo mahogany which ascends to a landing illuminated by a stained-glass window. The main rooms on the first floor are each finished in a different wood: Brazilian rosewood in one, walnut in another, mahogany in a third. The walls and ceilings are decorated with painted medallions showing scenes of Italian peasant life. The colors used by Giovanni Guidirini, the artist Austin employed, are as bright as the day they were applied, as is the gilt of the elaborate rococo cornices which surround every room.

The mansion came to the Victoria Society twenty years ago, in almost perfect condition, from the Holmes family, which had occupied it for many years. It is completely furnished in keeping with its elegance. Only a few of the pieces, however, belonged to the Morses. Most of the furnishings, which include many items of museum quality, have been acquired by gift or by purchase by the ladies of the Society. The house is open daily, except Mondays, during the summer.

52

Rhode Island Riches:

Nichols-Wanton-Hunter House

Roger Williams founded Rhode Island in 1636 as an island of tolerance between stiff-necked Massachusetts and Connecticut. A century later the mixture of free-thinkers in the little colony on Narragansett Bay was setting the pace for all New England in the manufacture of rum, the slave trade, and that legalized piracy known as privateering.

The architectural heritage of Rhode Island reflects the wealth that then poured in from the sea. The surviving homes and public buildings of these boom times are largely concentrated in Newport and on College Hill in Providence. Their urbane, sophisticated builders had come a long way from the medieval carpentry of the seventeenth century that produced that Rhode Island peculiarity, the "stone-ender." The most interesting of these early houses, in which a huge chimney forms an end wall, is the Eleazer Arnold home at Lincoln, just north of Providence; it is open during the summer months.

Before the Revolution Newport was the center of the lucrative "triangular trade." Thirty distilleries supplied the rum that helped buy the slaves in Africa, who then were shipped to the plantations of the South via the West Indies, where molasses to make more rum was obtained. The ships of Newport rivaled those of all American ports in general trade, as well as in sugar, rum, and slaves. The boldest merchants, when war offered an excuse, commissioned their ships as privateers.

For a time during the eighteenth century Boston and Philadelphia were the only American cities larger than Newport, but her trade was shattered by the Revolution and never returned. Industry and railroads later passed Newport by. The Colonial port, which had always been a resort for wealthy Southerners, waited decades for rediscovery by vacationing millionaires. The Southerners had returned early in the nineteenth century; Bostonians, New Yorkers, and Philadelphians by 1840.

The pre-Revolutionary elegance of the little, undisturbed island city is apparent in many buildings, especially in the Nichols-Wanton-Hunter house. Jonathan Nichols, Jr., deputy

In 1748 Jonathan Nichols, Jr., deputy governor of Rhode Island, built a mansion that was, within, one of the most luxurious in Newport. The pineapple carving — symbol of hospitality — over the doorway (*detail above*) is one of the few decorations on the dignified exterior. The house was successively owned by Nichols, Joseph Wanton, Jr., and William Hunter.

governor of Rhode Island and the owner of sixteen ships, built the mansion on Washington Street in 1748. It was bought six years later, after Nichols' death, by Joseph Wanton, Jr., who also served as deputy governor and fled to British-held New York during the Revolution. The house was confiscated and became the quarters of the ailing Admiral de Ternay, commander of the French fleet that arrived in Newport in 1780, who died there. William Hunter, a lawyer, graduate of Brown University, and an assistant secretary of state, was the owner for two decades early in the nineteenth century, until he became Senator from Rhode Island and moved to Washington. The house had been used as a convent when it was saved from destruction by the Preservation Society of Newport County twenty years ago.

The dignified, sparingly ornamented exterior of the mansion contrasts with the wealth of the interior. The walls, deep window seats, interior shutters, mantels, cornices, and cupboards are all magnificently executed painted pine woodwork. The paint in several rooms is grained to imitate either marble or decorative woods. The Preservation Society, when the house is open from June 1 to October 1 each year, furnishes the rooms with outstanding pieces by Newport's famous Colonial cabinetmakers, the Townsends and the Goddards, and silver and paintings by local artists and craftsmen.

The wealth from the sea flowed to Providence after the Revolution and resulted in the construction of larger, more impressive homes. John Brown's big brick mansion, built at 52 Power Street in 1786, looks exactly as the home of Providence's most important citizen should look. It was designed for him by his scholarly brother Joseph, who had a talent for architecture as well as astronomy and mechanics and whose skill as an amateur architect of the late Georgian period dominates old Providence. He also designed the handsome First Baptist Meeting House, built just before the Revolution, and his own handsome, baroque home, which is still one of the landmarks on South Main Street.

John was the oldest of the four Brown brothers, "the Cleverest Boy in Providence Town," he noted in one of his school books. They began as a team, outfitting privateers, and after the Revolution John operated on his own, sending one of the first vessels to open the China trade. John, Joseph, Nicholas, and Moses firmly planted the Browns in the affairs of Providence.

John's big house, which his brother ornamented with the first portico built in Providence, was the "most magnificent and elegant mansion" in America, John Quincy Adams recorded after his first visit. The interior is quite as impressive as the outside. The paneling used to ornament earlier mansions such as the Nichols-Wanton-Hunter house in Newport was replaced in the high-ceilinged rooms with elaborately carved pediments over the doorways, pilasters, and overmantel decoration. The house, which was enlarged by the family by the addition of a wing in later years, has been the headquarters and museum of the Rhode Island Historical Society since 1942 and is open Monday through Friday throughout the year, and Sunday afternoons during the summer.

New London's
Hempsted House

Joshua Hempsted was not the first of his name in New London, Connecticut, but the house he built in 1678 and the diary his son, Joshua II, kept from 1711 until 1758 reveal a great deal about the community the first Hempsted, Robert, helped found in 1646.

The Hempsted land was at first a fourteen-acre farm, well outside the town itself and only a quarter of a mile from salt water, but today the house is in the heart of New London, a mile or more from the deep harbor formed by the Thames River. A brook that ran by the door is buried deep in a culvert, and the traffic and commerce of the city flow all around. Hempsted House, however, has recovered its country look. The Antiquarian & Landmarks Society of Connecticut, at the time of its most recent restoration in 1959, obtained enough surrounding land to bring back a small piece of tree-shaded meadow, reconstruct a sweep-lift well, and plant shrubs and flowers that Joshua might have found familiar, and the diary of the younger Joshua has been most useful in furnishing the interior with items he enumerated. The house remained in the family until it was purchased from the heirs of poetess Anna Hempstead Branch in 1938, and some of the Hempsteds' crude Colonial furnishings had survived. A writing chair is notable among the family pieces. A high-back settle equipped with a reading stand, a folding bed, and a wood-castered baby walker illustrate early Yankee inventiveness.

Joshua II, who was a shipwright, carpenter, politician, and gravestone engraver as well as a farmer, described in detail many of the unusual aspects of the house, including the sliding diamond-paned casement windows in the second-floor bedroom. He removed the unusual gabled two-story "entrance porch" his father had built. This entranceway, and the tiny chamber above it, were rebuilt when the house was restored.

Hempsted House, like many in seventeenth-century New England, was built in stages. At first it had just the one big room on each floor to the right of the immense chimney. Joshua added two lean-tos — one at the back, where the north winds howled, and another to the

In 1678, in New London, Connecticut, Joshua Hempsted, son of a founder of the town, designed and built his own house. The gabled, two-story entrance "porch" and the rare attic dormer window were parts of the original structure. His grandson, Nathanael, added the right side of the house in 1728.

Nathan Hale (*above*) was a frequent visitor to the house and a friend of Stephen Hempsted, its owner during Revolutionary days. They were together shortly before Hale was captured and hanged behind the British lines.

The kitchen shows many rarities in early wrought iron, woodenware, and pewter. The herbs drying by the fireplace, a seventeenth-century cradle, and simple early furniture give a feeling of warmth and self-sufficiency.

right of the chimney for his office. It was his grandson, Nathanael, who demolished the office lean-to and added that side of the house in 1728.

In 1781 Benedict Arnold burned New London, but the Hempsted farm, perhaps because it was still on the outskirts of town, was spared and is now its oldest structure. It certainly would not have been spared if Arnold had known that it had been visited by Nathan Hale, who was a friend of Stephen Hempsted, its owner during the Revolutionary period. Stephen was with his friend in 1776 on Hale's journey behind British lines, where he was trapped and hanged. Stephen later received wounds that crippled him for life at the battle of Fort Griswold on Groton Heights, across the Thames from New London.

After the house was enlarged Joshua's big west room served as a schoolroom for the Hempsted children, in keeping with the New England tradition of using the big ground-floor chamber known as the "hall" for every aspect of family life. The walls of this room are unusually thick and insulated with a nogging of eel grass and sun-dried brick that can be seen through an aperture cut in an interior board. The huge summer beam across the middle of the ceiling, which supports the joists for the second floor, has unusually fine chamfered, or beveled, edges which terminate, as the beam reaches each side wall, with the familiar "lamb's tongue" stop. Typically, this is the extent of the architectural decoration the early New Englanders added to the interior of their homes.

The Hempsted house is open daily from mid-May to mid-October.

Old Stone House, Guilford

Religious faith has often shaped the course of history — and it played a leading role in the swift, permanent colonization of New England by settlers who were seeking not treasure but homes. The heavy hand of Britain's established church forced a steady stream of able, industrious dissenters across the Atlantic. Whole congregations accompanied their spiritual leaders on crowded little ships.

One of the most able of the leaders was the Reverend Henry Whitfield, who brought his flock to settle Guilford, Connecticut, in 1639. Whitfield, who had broken with the Church of England, brought families to America from his congregation in the town of Ockley and from neighboring congregations in Surrey and Kent. They landed at Quinnipiac (New Haven), where his friend John Davenport had established a colony, and then bought land from the Indians for their town midway between Quinnipiac and Saybrook, where another friend of Whitfield's, George Fenwick, had settled.

Whitfield and his congregation, beginning in the fall of that year, built a stone house, on a knoll at the edge of Long Island Sound, which is today the oldest stone dwelling erected by white men within the present boundaries of the United States. Only the wooden Fairbanks Homestead in Massachusetts, erected in 1637, and the Palace of the Governors in Santa Fe, New Mexico, built of adobe from 1610 to 1614, predate it.

Whitfield's house was a remarkably ambitious structure for the time and the place. It served as meetinghouse and fort for the twenty-five families who had accompanied him, and as a home for his wife Dorothy, seven of their nine children, and whatever servants they may have had. All this activity was confined within an L-shaped house almost forty feet long in each wing, two stories high, topped by a steeply pitched roof that covered a spacious attic. The stone walls, two feet thick, were superb for defensive purposes, but the labor required to quarry and erect them obviously outweighed the advantages in the opinion of Whitfield's neighbors and other colonists in New England, who preferred to build with wood. Even the

In 1639 the Reverend Henry Whitfield founded Guilford, Connecticut, and his congregation painstakingly built what is today the oldest stone dwelling erected by white men in the United States. Friendly Menuncabeck Indians carried the stones to the building site of the future meetinghouse and fort. The structure is of unusual size and importance, English Gothic in appearance, with thick walls, small windows, massive chimneys, and a steep roof.

A square staircase winds to the second floor, which contains two sleeping chambers and the study (*above*), with Whitfield's writing table and Bible and an architecturally unique corner window.

mortar to bind the stone was a problem, because of the lack of limestone. This was solved at Guilford by mixing pulverized burned oyster shells with clay.

The interior of the house was framed with oak beams, with pine and whitewood used for partitions. The inside dimensions of the great hall on the first floor are thirty-three by fifteen feet. This is believed to have been the original house, to which the kitchen ell was added. The fireplaces at each end are ten feet wide. A separate tower was built to contain the stairs to the second floor, which is divided into two rooms with a ladderlike stairs in a hall between them to reach the attic above.

Whitfield left his home and congregation to return to England in 1650; his wife and children remained in Guilford. No documents survive to explain his departure, but his arrival in England coincided with the rise of Oliver Cromwell and political security for the Puritans. He died in England in 1657 and is buried at Winchester.

When Mrs. Whitfield returned to England in 1659 the house was sold. During the next two hundred and thirty years it had a succession of owners and was occupied most of the time by tenant farmers. The State of Connecticut bought Whitfield's house in 1889, and it was opened as a museum in 1902 under the auspices of the Colonial Dames of America, Connecticut Chapter. A painstaking restoration, based on Guilford's town records and an almost stone-by-stone dissection of the house, was begun in 1930, for Old Stone House, as it was known by then, had been gutted by fire in 1868, and the surviving stone walls had been covered with stucco; the rebuilt interior had only a limited resemblance to its original appearance. About one-third of the building as it stands is entirely original — notably, the chimney and wall at the north end of the structure. The strange hinged wood partition, which can be lowered to divide the great hall into two rooms, is a duplicate of similar dividers found in the larger medieval homes. Something of the sort must have existed to keep the interior warm for the family and yet permit use of the entire room when Whitfield preached to his congregation or conferred with them about the town's civic affairs.

A Board of Trustees from Guilford oversees the maintenance of the house for the state. The furnishings include typical seventeenth-century articles — a chair that belonged to a seventeenth-century governor, William Leete, and a massive table from the same period — a gift from the late J. Frederick Kelly, the architect who directed the restoration of the house. A typical early American herb garden is maintained in a walled area outside the kitchen door. The house is surrounded by open meadow. It is open to the public daily, but closed from mid-December to mid-January.

Wethersfield:

Buttolph-Williams House
&
Webb House

The first settlement in Connecticut was not along the coast but far up the Connecticut River at Wethersfield, which is a suburb of Hartford today. A Captain John Oldham ventured up "ye Great River" to this place where the hills flattened out into fertile meadows. His enthusiasm for this tillable, accessible soil, when he returned to Massachusetts Bay, led to the organization of a colony called The Adventurers, who bought land from the Indians at Wethersfield in 1634. The remote settlement was nearly wiped out by an Indian raiding party in its third year, but the advantage of excellent farmland at the edge of navigable water brought a quick recovery. Wethersfield prospered through the seventeenth and eighteenth centuries but was not caught up in the industrial boom that followed. The result is a twentieth-century residential town filled with handsome old houses — one hundred and forty of them predating 1800.

One museum dwelling — the Buttolph-Williams house — is typical of the substantial homes the seventeenth-century settlers built. It is the familiar medieval post and girt construction, sheathed with riven oak clapboards. The heavy posts that rise from the foundation sill to the second floor end in a projecting carved bracket, or corbel, so that the upper story of the house overhangs the first floor by four inches. The overhang, which was common practice in medieval building, occurs on some early New England homes and is frequently observed in Europe. The most pronounced overhangs were achieved by having the second-floor girts project a foot or more beyond the posts that supported them.

David Buttolph built the house in 1692, the year of his well-to-do father's death. It was a large house for the times — almost a mansion — and David, who was only twenty-four, is believed to have purchased the frame, perhaps from a neighbor whose home had been wrecked by a disastrous flood that is known to have swept the Connecticut Valley that year. He did not live in the house long. Buttolph, a cordwainer, moved from Wethersfield in 1698 to set up a tannery in Simsbury.

The Buttolph-Williams house (*above*) is typical of the handsome and sturdy dwellings erected in the fertile, remote inlands. David Buttolph built his house in 1692 in Wethersfield, the first settlement in Connecticut. The second-story overhang is a familiar medieval practice.

"Ye Greate Kitchin," the heart of the household, is known as the most completely equipped seventeenth-century kitchen in the nation. It contains early woodenwares, furniture, and even a jack and weights listed in a 1692 inventory.

The Joseph Webb house (*below*), built in 1752, is the largest and finest eighteenth-century Wethersfield house. Its doorway is columned and pedimented, and there is exquisite Georgian woodwork in all the rooms. Washington stayed here, perhaps because Joseph's son, Samuel, was his private secretary. The Comte de Rochambeau used the chamber (*above*) bearing his name, during the historic Yorktown Conference in May 1781 at which the final British defeat was plotted.

The house, after having a succession of owners, was bought by Daniel Williams in 1721 and remained in his family for one hundred and forty years. The Williamses were succeeded by the Vibert family, from whom it was acquired by the Antiquarian & Landmarks Society of Connecticut in 1947. The house is open to the public daily from mid-May to mid-October. Wethersfield's seventeenth-century landmark is outstanding for the care with which it has been restored and furnished with objects similar to those the Buttolphs used.

The first-floor parlor is furnished with finer pieces — pewter chargers and candlesticks and English delftware, which was popular in America in the seventeenth century. The furniture includes a gate-leg table with leather hinges, slat- and bannister-back chairs, a court cupboard and trestle table, both of seventeenth-century New England manufacture, and a sunflower-and-tulip carved chest with the date 1672 inscribed upon it.

Unusual architectural and decorative features include a delightful little winding staircase in the entrance "porch" which is ornamented with a well-turned newel post and six little balusters only eight inches high — a bit of original craftsmanship as strikingly Jacobean as the leaded casement windows, which are not original, but faithful reproductions. Massive bolection moldings around two of the big fireplaces are part of the woodwork the Buttolphs installed. Baseboards in the parlor are stained almost black with pokeberry juice, as was customary in early houses. Woodwork in the bedchamber above the parlor is colored with a reddish buttermilk paint known as "dragon's blood." Doors, trim, and moldings in this room are all unchanged from the time the house was built.

The Buttolph-Williams house is on Broad Street. A block west, on Main Street, you step into the second half of the eighteenth century, confronted by three fine old houses owned by the Connecticut Chapter of the Colonial Dames. The Joseph Webb house, built in 1752 and the center of the group, is flanked on the right by the Isaac Stevens house, built in 1789, and on the left by the home of Silas Deane, built in 1766. One of the military campaigns that helped inaugurate the Revolution was planned in the home of Deane, a prominent patriot and statesman; it was headquarters for the Connecticut men who captured Fort Ticonderoga in 1775. The largest and finest of the three is the Webb house, famous for its occupancy by George Washington while he and the Comte de Rochambeau plotted the Yorktown campaign, which resulted in the surrender of the British and the end of the Revolutionary War.

The Webb house boasts a columned and pedimented doorway and exquisite Georgian woodwork in all its rooms. It is furnished with antiques of the period, reflecting a fashion that remains unexcelled for good taste and livability to this day. The red flock wallpaper in the bedroom used by General Washington is a French import, said to have been installed by Mrs. Webb in anticipation of the visit of her distinguished guest. Washington's use of the house was arranged by his private secretary, Samuel Webb, son of the builder.

Both the Webb and the Stevens houses are open the year round, except Sundays. The Stevens dwelling is notable for having been in the possession of one family for one hundred and seventy years and is furnished with many relics of the family. Restoration and furnishing of Silas Deane's home is nearing completion.

II

NEW YORK
AND THE
HUDSON VALLEY

New York City, 1797.

NEW YORK
AND THE
HUDSON VALLEY

There are two myths associated with the earliest American homes that architectural historians have debunked in recent years. One is the notion that all pioneers lived in log cabins. There is ample evidence that the early colonists, with the possible exception of the Swedes, did not know how to construct them. The other myth has its origin in the Hudson Valley, where gambrel-roof houses near New York City popularized a design mistakenly known as Dutch Colonial. In fact, the so-called Dutch Colonial suburban homes, built in great numbers in the early 1900s, are neither Dutch nor Colonial; the design came to America with Flemish immigrants who erected their farm homes after, and not before, the Revolution.

The Flemish settlers in northern New Jersey were the aftermath of an influx from the Low Countries to the Hudson Valley that began in 1624, when the Dutch captain Cornelius May landed nearly a score of Walloon families at an already fortified place far up the river which in time became Albany. Others had left his ship to found New Amsterdam, now New York, on the island of Manhattan.

The Dutch, the Walloons, and the other Protestant refugees who came from Holland to New Netherlands made their own bricks, cut stone and timbers, and erected dwellings which merit description as Dutch Colonial. Few of those built in the seventeenth century remain, but such villages as Hurley and New Paltz today contain many homes that reflect the Low Country origin of their builders. Two of the houses mentioned in the following pages — Fort Crailo and the Bronck house — look as if they had been lifted bodily from Holland. Their steeply pitched roofs and picturesque brick gables have no relation to the flaring, bell-shaped gambrels of the later Flemish homes.

Although the Duke of York, later to become King James II, claimed and named New York in 1664, the Dutch influence persisted. Even Manhattan, until a great fire swept the city during the Revolution, retained the architectural character of New Amsterdam. No trace of the Dutch settlement has remained on the island, but residents can get an idea of what once existed by crossing the East River to view the Old Stone House at Gowanus, reconstructed at Third Avenue and Fifth Street in Brooklyn. But British architectural ideas captured the fancy of the well-to-do, the Dutch included, in the eighteenth century. The owners of the great manors led the way into the Georgian era. Philipse Manor in Yonkers and the Schuyler mansion in Albany are examples of the architectural elegance commanded by a handful of wealthy New Yorkers.

Their riches derived from the patroon system inaugurated by the Dutch. Vast manors, in which whole villages and countless farms paid rent, persisted well into the nineteenth century, but the patroons never established themselves firmly outside the Hudson Valley. Dutch attempts to colonize the Connecticut and Delaware Valleys failed. The Mohawk Valley belonged to fierce and well-organized Indian tribes, and the wilderness north and west was territory better known to the French coming from the Saint Lawrence and the Great Lakes.

English penetration of the Mohawk frontier came in the eighteenth century. Johnson Hall, erected in 1763 at Johnstown, New York, by Sir William Johnson, Britain's Superintendent of Indian Affairs for the Northern Colonies, survives as a reminder of England's cultivation of the redskins — the Six Nations in particular. That alliance led to fearful butchery of American settlers during the Revolution, reviving the Indian terror instigated by the French a generation earlier. The Georgian mansion is flanked by a stone blockhouse, which Sir William found useful on occasion in dealing with his savage allies.

West of Johnstown, at Little Falls, is a more modest brick home built in 1764 by General Nicholas Herkimer, the "Old Honikol" from the backwoods who routed the British and the Indians at Oriskany in 1777. His house is more English than German, but Old Honikol's ancestry is delightfully evident in a little note that survived him. "Bles do led de berer half as manne brics for a schimle as hie wants an so duing ye wil oblege your humble Sv. Nicholas Herchmer," he wrote at the time he was building his house.

The ambitions of France in New York have survived at Fort Niagara in a stone fort disguised as a dwelling and trading post, built in 1726. The commander of this important post on the French route to the Ohio and the Mississippi did not want to alarm his Indian friends and requested his engineer, one Gaspard Chaussegros de Léry, to design a bastion which would have the appearance of a residential trading post. "Instead of wooden partitions I have built heavy walls and paved all the floors with flat stone," de Léry later reported in his description of the structure, which became known as "the castle."

France lost "the castle" to the English after a siege in 1759, and they, in turn, held it until long after the Revolution. The British left Fort Niagara in 1796, returning during the War of 1812 for a final brief stay.

The dreams and schemes of many nationalities can be read in the structures that survive in the Empire State.

Fort Crailo, Rensselaer

The Dutch settlement of the Hudson Valley did not go well in its first five years. New Amsterdam at the river's mouth and Fort Orange at the head of navigation were simply trading posts and not self-sufficient communities.

In 1629, therefore, the West India Company established the patroon system to grant huge estates along the river to stockholders who would populate the land with farmer tenants. Originally, two patroonships were planned along the Hudson. The one that survived from that early date and grew until the manor held all the land for forty-eight miles on both sides of the upper Hudson was established by Kiliaen Van Rensselaer, an Amsterdam diamond merchant.

Kiliaen never left his counting house to visit the lands that brought his family great wealth, but his cousin, Arent Van Curler, came to America in 1638 and built a manor house at *Greenen Bosch*, now Rensselaer. That structure has vanished, but the dwelling known as Fort Crailo is believed to have been erected on the same site. Hendrick Van Rensselaer built Fort Crailo in 1704 and incorporated into the foundation two stones in which the initials KVR and the date 1642 are carved. Fort Crailo was given to the State of New York by a descendant of patroon Kiliaen in 1924.

The interior of the main part of the house has been restored in medieval Dutch style to match the striking seventeenth-century exterior, which is brick, laid in Dutch cross bond, with leaded casement windows and a deeply pitched tile roof. The bricks on the gable ends are laid in a strange and delightful slanting pattern beneath the heavy coping that rises to the chimney, a device popular with medieval Flemish masons and described by the Dutch as "mouse-tooth" finish. These patterns, which occur in only a handful of early brick houses along the upper Hudson, also ornament the gables of Judge Leonard Bronck's farm home, built in 1738 at West Coxsackie adjacent to a smaller stone dwelling erected in 1663 by his ancestor Pieter. The houses are maintained as a museum by the Greene County Historical

Kiliaen Van Rensselaer ordered Fort Crailo built in 1704 to serve as an administrative center for the eastern branch of his patroonship along the Hudson, which he ran from Amsterdam. The handsomely patterned original brick walls are matched by the medieval Dutch character of the restored interior. Rooms are paneled in vertical beaded pine boards and have heavy plank floors. Loopholes for defense appear in the heavy walls. Much tradition is associated with the Fort, where, it is said, "Yankee Doodle" was written.

Society and open during summer months. Pieter's father, Jan, who first settled in New Amsterdam, gave his name to the Bronx borough of New York.

Hendrick Van Rensselaer incorporated one strictly American feature in his manor. Loopholes for defense were built into the heavy brick walls, most likely with the warlike Iroquois just west of the Van Rensselaer lands in mind. One of these loopholes through the original rear wall can be seen inside the rear wing of the house, a 1762 addition finished in the Georgian manner. The name of the fortress dwelling, Crailo, was taken from a Van Rensselaer estate in Holland.

The rooms, as restored, are paneled in vertical beaded pine boards. The floors are heavy planks, set on widely spaced joists, and a "ship's ladder" stairs rises to the second floor from the center hall. The beds, following Dutch custom, are incredibly short "built-in" enclosures. The furnishings have been carefully selected to include only those pieces, mostly of Dutch origin, which would have been found in the house when it served the Van Rensselaers as the manor for that part of their lands on the east side of the Hudson.

Today, Fort Crailo is separated from the river's edge by a line of buildings; a primitive painting of the house and the farm that surrounded it one hundred and fifty years ago hangs in the wing. The proximity of the structure to the water fosters the belief that an escape tunnel once extended to the bank of the Hudson from the basement. Strange vaulted rooms in the same area are said to be slave pens.

The most intriguing legend connected with Fort Crailo is that "Yankee Doodle" was written at the Van Rensselaer manor. When a Colonial army was assembled at Rensselaer in 1758 to march with British troops under Sir Robert Abercromby against the French fortress at Ticonderoga, a British army surgeon, Dr. Richard Shuckburgh, is said to have sat on the curbing of the stone-walled well in the yard behind Fort Crailo and penned the words of "Yankee Doodle" to mock the Colonials arriving from New England. His verses, set to an Old World tune, furnished a marching song that rallied Americans and taunted the British when the Revolution began.

Fort Crailo, which is administered by New York as a historic site, is open the year round.

General Philip Schuyler — engraving by W. W. Rice after a painting by Chappel.

Schuyler's Albany Mansion

General Philip Schuyler's impressive Georgian home at Albany is known as "The Pastures." When it was completed in 1762, the brick mansion stood just outside the town, high above green pastures dropping away to the Hudson. The house was almost directly across the river from tile-roofed Fort Crailo, home of the general's wife, "Sweet Kitty" Van Rensselaer.

Mrs. Schuyler brought the house to completion. The general, then major, was in London on a military mission. He spent a great deal of his time abroad buying wallpaper and draperies for the new house, recording the purchases in lists that have survived. Catherine Schuyler supervised their installation and selected the rich blues, yellows, and greens used on the woodwork throughout the house, while General John Bradstreet, a friend of the Schuylers, supervised the carpenters, masons, and other craftsmen. The lumber for The Pastures came from the Schuyler estate upriver at Old Saratoga, now known as Schuylerville, the location of the general's country home, recently restored by the National Park Service.

The loss and rebuilding of that home during the Revolution and a related episode at The Pastures reveal a great deal about the manorial lives of the wealthy and courtly Schuylers. The new Schuylerville house was a replacement for one which was burned by the British general "Gentleman Johnny" Burgoyne shortly before he was forced to surrender at

79

General Philip Schuyler's impressive Georgian mansion, in Albany, was completed in 1762. Architecturally it is notable for its generous dimensions and the Chippendale railing surrounding the hipped roof, a device later copied by many. The hexagonal porch was added in the late eighteenth century.

Betsy Schuyler Hamilton — detail of a painting by Ralph Earl.

Alexander Hamilton — painting by Constantino Brumidi.

The interior reflects the splendor and gaiety of the life of the Schuyler family. Mrs. Schuyler selected rich Prussian blues, Venetian reds, yellows, and greens for the woodwork, and the general brought wallpapers and draperies from abroad. Schuyler's daughter Betsy married Alexander Hamilton in 1780 in the handsomely paneled parlor known today as the Hamilton Room.

Saratoga. Schuyler hustled slaves and prisoners of war to rebuild at Schuylerville, and at the same time extended a welcome at The Pastures to Burgoyne as a prisoner. His forgiving host, the British general later reported, "much to my surprise presented me to Mrs. Schuyler and her family; and in General Schuyler's house I remained during the whole of my stay in Albany, with a table of more than twenty covers for me and my friends, and every other demonstration of hospitality." Burgoyne, through the fortunes of war, got a generous sample of the Schuyler hospitality, which was well known to almost every important figure in the young nation.

Sweet Kitty's daughters were as charming as their mother. Betsy, whom one of Washington's aides described as "A Brunette with the most good natured lovely dark eyes I ever saw," married Alexander Hamilton at The Pastures in 1780. The ceremony took place in the handsomely paneled parlor known today as the Hamilton Room, finished with marble facing on the fireplace and gleaming brass door locks which the general had had shipped from London when he was a young man.

The kitchen, slave quarters, barns, and other outbuildings which supported the Schuylers' rich life were lost as the city engulfed The Pastures. The mansion was used as an orphan asylum just before its purchase by the state in 1911. Restoration has included the return of many family possessions — furniture, portraits, silver, even articles of clothing. The rooms are decorated as Catherine Schuyler decreed in the beginning. Paints reproduce the colors of the first coats found on the woodwork; the draperies are modern reproductions of those that her husband bought abroad.

The Pastures is notable, architecturally, both for its generous dimensions — the structure is sixty-three feet long — and for the Chippendale railing that surrounds the hipped roof at its terminus just above the eaves. This ornamentation, if installed at the time the house was built, was an experiment American builders did not copy for a generation. Balustrades on Georgian houses occurred only at the apex of the structure, surrounding a roof-deck. Their use above the eaves did not become popular until the Federal period.

The Schuyler mansion is maintained as a museum by New York State and open the year round.

Washington's Dutch Colonial Headquarters

The big, barnlike house where Washington waited out the last year of the Revolution, from 1782 to 1783, commands a magnificent view of the Hudson in its passage through the mountains to reach New York harbor and the sea. Here, at Newburgh, the Continental army stood over the British in New York City while Europe debated the terms of peace.

The commander-in-chief's headquarters was the farm home of Tryntje Hasbrouck, a widow. The land had been bought by Mrs. Elsie Hasbrouck of New Paltz for her son Jonathan in March 1749. In 1750 Jonathan built the northeast portion of the house and the following year married Catherine (Tryntje) Dubois. In 1754 he bought the property from his mother and lived there for the next twenty-six years until his death, when the house passed into the possession of his widow, Tryntje.

Washington, in accepting his headquarters from a woman named Tryntje, surely must have thought of it as a Dutch home. It was unlike any dwelling he had known in Virginia, or in any of the other colonies, for that matter. The Marquis de Chastellux, after a visit in 1782, said of the house: "The largest room in it (which was the proprietor's parlor for his family, and which General Washington has converted into his dining-room) is in truth tolerably spacious, but it has seven doors and only one window. The chimney, or rather the chimney back, is against the wall; so that there is in fact but one vent for smoke, and the fire is in the room itself." The marquis was describing a hood fireplace, a primitive arrangement in which the smoke, instead of being channeled within walls of brick or stone, was allowed to find its way up into the chimney above, which began at ceiling height. The room with seven doors was the earliest part of the house Jonathan Hasbrouck built, and his hood fireplace is a unique survival of a heating and cooking arrangement believed to have existed in many of the early "Dutch" Colonial houses.

If the Marquis de Castellux had ventured up into the attic of the Hasbrouck house he would have seen another architectural curiosity worth noting in his journal. The maze of

Engraving of George Washington after
a painting by Colonel John Trumbull.

The room of one window and seven doors is
the largest and was used by Washington for
dining and receptions. The hooded fireplace,
common in early Colonial houses, is one of
the very few that have survived in original
form.

Jonathan Hasbrouck built his "Dutch Colonial" house in 1750 in Newburgh, New York. It shows French, English, and Dutch influences. The interior woodwork is Georgian. The house became General Washington's headquarters from 1782 to 1783. Here he was notified of the end of hostilities and was asked to form a new government.

bracing timbers, cross members, and rafters, notched and pegged to support the towering roof, is best described as fantastic.

"Dutch Colonial" is a handy label for the famous old house in Newburgh, but it leaves a lot unsaid. The story of the man who built it is more revealing of the French origins of some of the settlers who are labeled "Dutch." Jonathan Hasbrouck came from New Paltz, a little village north of Newburgh established by the French-speaking Hasbroucks and other Walloon families in 1678. They were Huguenots driven from France to the Rhine, then brought to New Netherlands with the Dutch. They settled first at the town of Hurley. In 1712 Jonathan's uncle, Jean Hasbrouck, had built a fieldstone house at New Paltz which looks like a smaller edition of the Newburgh Headquarters. It is maintained as a museum by the Huguenot Historical Society. A visit to the loft reveals the French-Dutch bracing that Jonathan copied in the latticework of timbers with which he supported the roof of his house at Newburgh.

The interior woodwork of the house at Newburgh is Georgian, not Dutch. Jonathan no doubt "modernized" when additions were built, but the trim of the original structure indicated that he, like other prosperous Colonials in the mid-eighteenth century, was influenced by British ideas. He was a step ahead of his church in adopting British ways. The Dutch Reformed congregation in New Paltz continued services in French until just about the time Jonathan moved to Newburgh, and then used the Dutch language until well after the Revolution, when English was adopted.

Washington occupied the Hasbrouck house from April 1782 to August of the following year, when the troops camped at nearby Temple Hill were either furloughed or transferred downriver to West Point. The months of inaction on the hillside above the Hudson were difficult for him and for the restless army. The commander-in-chief had to contend with soldiers who were not receiving either their full pay or proper rations, and with officers who wanted to take over from the Congress. One of them, Colonel Lewis Nicola, proposed naming Washington "King" — an idea that the future first President rejected in a famous letter of rebuke. The Order of the Purple Heart was established by Washington's order from his headquarters at Newburgh.

The State of New York purchased the house from the Hasbrouck family in 1849, and in so doing marked the beginning, nearly a decade earlier than elsewhere, of historic preservation in America. Carpenter's Hall, where the first Continental Congress met in Philadelphia, was next opened to the public in 1857, and Mount Vernon was acquired by its famous Ladies' Association in 1858. The Hasbrouck house and an adjoining museum are open the year round.

Portrait of States Morris Dyckman; attributed to John Trumbull.

Boscobel

The Hudson Valley is a land of vistas, a tumble of pleasant hills and accessible mountains looking down upon the deep river that splits them apart. For the past three hundred years men have perched an infinite variety of homes, from cottage to castle, on vantage points overlooking the shining waterway. The handsomest, perhaps, is the house called Boscobel. Certainly it commands the finest vista of all in its present location on a plateau at Garrison, New York, two hundred feet above the river. Here the Hudson, circling east below Mount Beacon, turns straight south through the mountains to the Tappan Zee.

Boscobel was created in the style of the Scottish architect Robert Adam by States Morris Dyckman, who was born on a Hudson River farm in 1755. Dyckman, of Dutch ancestry, found a career in the Quartermaster Corps of the British army and spent many years abroad. But he dreamed of living with his family in America in a home overlooking the Hudson. He had in mind a house in the latest English style, named for an estate in Shropshire, England, where Charles II took refuge from Cromwell after the Battle of Worcester.

Dyckman's dream began to take form shortly after 1800, when he started construction of Boscobel on Montross Point, just south of Peekskill. The plan was derived from Robert Adam, England's master of classic grace. Dyckman was well acquainted with Robert's nephew William and bought in England mantels and many of the embellishments for his new home. But States Dyckman died in 1806, before his dream was fully realized. His widow, Elizabeth, had to complete the mansion and conduct the business of the farm, which was to remain in the family for generations.

The day came, however, when Dyckman's dream home was abandoned. In the 1920s the land on Montross Point was purchased for park purposes. The house was to be destroyed, but it was saved by public protest. Nearly a quarter-century later, however, when

87

Elizabeth Dyckman.

Boscobel is considered the finest example of Robert Adam's style in America, and was built by States Morris Dyckman shortly after 1800. It originally stood on Montross Point, south of Peekskill, but was stored away piece by piece to save it from destruction, and later rebuilt at Garrison.

88

the site was obtained by the Veterans' Administration for a new hospital, similar protest proved unavailing; the house was sold to a wrecker to be cleared away. But States Dyckman's dream refused to die. His vision of an Adam mansion overlooking the Hudson was revived in the plans of a few New Yorkers, inspired by author Carl Carmer, who banded together to save the house. They bought the frame structure, stored it away, piece by piece, and a few years later rebuilt Boscobel at Garrison, fifteen miles north of its original location. DeWitt and Lila Acheson Wallace, founders of the *Reader's Digest*, took the lead in the rebirth of Boscobel, which is maintained by a foundation established in the name of the magazine.

The site at Garrison is large and includes the outbuildings, orchards, and gardens that would have been found surrounding the mansion of a wealthy Hudson River farmer in the early years of the Republic. Boscobel's big front windows and porches look south across the deep valley to West Point on the Hudson's west shore. A sweep of lawn extends from the house to the abrupt rim of the hillside.

The façade Boscobel presents to the Hudson is not only exquisite in its classical treatment but the equal in glass area of many contemporary homes with "window walls" facing the south. Adam and the American architects and builders of our Federal period enormously increased the scale of wall openings. Glass was more readily available in larger sizes suitable for expanded surfaces and for bringing additional light to interior space.

The interior of Boscobel is almost dictated by the front façade. The entrance hall fills the space behind the first-floor porch and extends to the rear of the house, where a wide staircase rises to a landing beneath a large Palladian window. Stairs return toward the front from each end of the landing to a second-floor center hall. A drawing room and music room occupy one side bay of the first floor; a dining room, and a plate and china closet the other. The kitchen is in the basement. The second floor is devoted to bedrooms except for the space above the upper porch, where States Dyckman planned his library.

The present furnishing of the house is the ultimate realization of Dyckman's dream — an assembly of Adam-influenced pieces that might even have been beyond his means, had he lived. The architecturally impressive entrance hall, for instance, is enhanced by a large blue-flowered Moorfield carpet designed by Robert Adam, a Waterford chandelier, and Adam pier glass mirrors on the side walls. Every room in the house has been furnished with equal regard for the finest that was available, abroad and in America, in Dyckman's time.

Only a few objects associated with States Dyckman or his family are in the house. But he recorded the items he bought in England — books, china, glass, and silver — and a great deal of his additional planning for Boscobel in papers that survived him and were given to the foundation to guide its restoration.

Boscobel is open throughout the year, except Tuesdays and Wednesdays.

Morris-Jumel Mansion

Only one pre-Revolutionary dwelling has escaped the wrecking crews on Manhattan Island. It is the city-owned Morris-Jumel Mansion at One hundred and sixty-first Street, overlooking the Harlem River — an architecturally distinguished survival of New York's eighteenth-century aristocracy and of Washington's losing battle to prevent British occupation of the city.

Roger Morris, a member of New York's Legislative Council, built the house in 1765 on land that had been advertised in the *Mercury* as "A Pleasant situated Farm, on the Road leading to King's Bridge, in the Township of Harlem . . . commands the finest prospect in the whole Country: the Land runs from River to River: there is Fishing, Oystering, and Clamming at either end." He had married the beautiful, wealthy Mary Philipse, sister of

"The Reception to Governor Franklin," painted by John Ward Dunsmore, represents the first important occasion to take place in the newly built Morris Mansion. Roger Morris, his wife, Mary, and Governor Franklin are at center.

The Morris-Jumel mansion, Manhattan's only surviving pre-Revolutionary dwelling, was built by Roger Morris in 1765 to overlook the Harlem River. The rare Chinese-lattice roof rail and giant entrance portico forecast changes in the Georgian style. In 1810 the house was acquired by the wealthy merchant Stephen Jumel, whose illustrious wife added legend to history.

Colonel Roger Morris,
by Benjamin West.

In September 1776 Washington, a frequent caller, occupied the mansion and established his command in the octagonal first-floor room at the rear of the house.

Madame Stephen Jumel,
by Charles de Saint-Mémin.

Frederick Philipse III, in 1758. (The wedding, fabled for its brilliance, took place in the East Parlor of Philipse Manor, a richly decorated room in the big mansion at Yonkers that is a state museum today.) Mary, better known as Polly, had received a great deal of attention before her marriage from a young officer, George Washington.

Washington spent five weeks in the Morris mansion on Harlem Heights, but not until both Roger and Mary and their children had left. The Morrises and the Philipses were not interested in independence from the king. Morris had sailed to England in 1775, and his wife and children went to live at Philipse Manor. The commander-in-chief occupied the mansion in September 1776 to oversee his troops' withdrawal from Manhattan, which he had then decided to abandon to the British. His command was established in the unusual octagonal room on the first floor of the dwelling. This architectural treatment at the rear of the house is as advanced, for the period in which it was built, as the stately portico that ornaments the front. The four slender Doric columns supporting a roof-high pediment create a façade graceful enough to have been designed well after the Revolution rather than twenty years before.

The house is frame, with siding rusticated to give the appearance of masonry, quoined at the four corners. A latticework railing surrounds a deck at the peak of its low-hipped roof. Kitchen, laundry, and servants' quarters were all contained in the Morrises' basement, and they had twelve bedrooms available for family and guests in the second floor and attic.

Washington is said to have watched the final British and Hessian assault on the Heights from the house and to have returned across the Hudson to the American position at Fort Lee only minutes before the Morris home was seized by the king's men. The British Union Jack thereafter replaced the early American flag Washington had flown, which had the familiar thirteen red and white stripes but a small Union Jack in the space where the stars were later to appear.

The British paid rent to Morris for their use of the mansion. His property was confiscated after the Revolution, and the house was used as both a farm home and a tavern until it was acquired by a wealthy merchant, Stephen Jumel, in 1810. Madame Jumel, who was widowed in 1832 was a fabulous hostess and became famous for the parties held at her historic home. She married Aaron Burr when he was seventy-eight, two years before he died, and survived him by twenty-nine years. Her eccentricities before her death in 1865, which included maintenance of a private army that paraded daily at the mansion, added to the legend her parties had begun.

The Morris-Jumel mansion had a succession of owners until its acquisition by the City of New York in 1903. Restoration, in which the Daughters of the American Revolution cooperated with the city, required many years. The house is open throughout the year, except Mondays.

III

THE DELAWARE VALLEY

Court House and Centre Square, Easton, 1835.

THE

DELAWARE VALLEY

William Penn's "holy experiment" got a late start in the New World, half a century after Englishmen were firmly planted in New England and in Virginia. But the settlers who poured into Pennsylvania soon caught up. Even the Dutch and the Swedes, who had come to the banks of the Delaware earlier, found in Penn's Province a climate of tolerance and opportunity, centered in his "city of brotherly love." By the middle of the eighteenth century Philadelphia was the second-largest city in the English-speaking world.

The architectural heritage of the Delaware Valley is predominantly English, despite the Swedes, the Dutch, and the Germans who came with Penn. Georgian ideas influenced the builders of the more substantial surviving homes, which were erected after 1700 when the owners, whatever their ancestry, were happily prospering in Penn's melting pot. This is evident in all the houses described on subsequent pages.

The exceptions are few. The little house where John Morton, a signer of the Declaration of Independence, was born is a seventeenth-century log cabin — one of the homes built by Swedish settlers, who are thought to have introduced the log construction subsequently employed by pioneers from coast to coast. Morton's great-grandfather from Sweden, Morton Mortenson, erected part of the dwelling in 1654. A second section was added in 1698. At that stage the Morton home became a typical "dog-trot" dwelling — two one-room log cabins separated by an areaway, but all under one roof. The center areaway, or dog-trot, was walled in with stone by the family more than one hundred years later. Mortenson's logs, incidentally, are not round. The timbers were shaped with an adz into heavy planks similar to those used in the garrison houses of New England.

The Morton homestead, now a state property, is on the bank of Darby Creek, close to the Delaware River, where Governor Johan Printz established the capital of New Sweden in 1643. Only the foundations of his Prinzhof remain. The site and cabin are just south of the present limits of Philadelphia.

Two small churches built along the Delaware by Swedish congregations at the end of the seventeenth century reflect their antecedents, though both are Episcopal today. Holy Trinity, in Wilmington, was completed in 1699, and Old Swedes', or Gloria Dei, in Philadelphia, a year later. Holy Trinity is of stone, Gloria Dei, of brick.

Philadelphia became a city of brick, where crowded rows of houses duplicated those in London and other British communities. Brick also was used east of the Delaware in the flatlands of New Jersey. West of the river the English, Welsh, and German farmers who cleared rich little valleys and rolling uplands built with the readily available field-stone, often plastering and whitewashing the rubble walls. A single room, with attic above, generally was the original dwelling, which later became a wing when a larger two-story structure was built adjoining it. The design has been copied in countless suburbs.

The German-Americans of the eighteenth century soon modified the medieval building practices of their homeland to meet conditions and customs in America. There are isolated relics of huts built of squared logs, or with half-timbered walls, but the early farm homes that survive are for the most part field-stone. Many are ornamented with a pent eave, a projecting shed just above the first-floor windows and doorways that often circles the entire house. Grumblethorpe, on page 105, is typical in its design.

Two groups of communal buildings erected by religious sects in eastern Pennsylvania are the most striking survival of German medieval architectural practices. The Moravian Seminary at Bethlehem still occupies the stone Sisters House, an eighteenth-century dormitory which has not one but two levels of little dormer windows projecting from the long slope of its steep, high roof. At Ephrata the State of Pennsylvania maintains the strange buildings that housed the colony established by Conrad Beisel, mystic and musician. The Saron, a three-story frame structure containing sixty-two rooms for the women who once lived beneath its immense shingled roof, is straight out of the Reformation, though built about 1740. Heavy framing timbers make a maze of the interior. The wood-sheathed walls are filled, and well insulated, with clay nogging.

The contrast between this medieval structure and the Georgian elegance of Philadelphia buildings such as the Provincial State House (better known as Independence Hall) makes it difficult to believe that they were all built at the same time. Beisel's followers were more than a century behind the members of Philadelphia's Carpenters' Company, the craftsmen who not only finished the homes and public buildings of the Colonial period, but in most instances designed them.

The handsome little headquarters of the Carpenters is one of the historic shrines in Philadelphia's Independence National Historical Park. Carpenters' Hall was the meeting place of the first Continental Congress in 1774, when the Colonies united on a course that led to conflict and freedom for America. It also was an architectural fountainhead. The origins of Georgian and Federal-period construction are displayed there today in the master carpenters' design books, schedules of work to be performed, and prices to be charged, and in the tools they employed. They built the city in which the nation was born.

100

William Bartram — oil painting
by Charles Willson Peale, 1807.

Bartram's
Garden Home

One of the remarkable men of the eighteenth century who contributed much to the heritage of America was a Pennsylvania farmer named John Bartram. Bartram never participated in military maneuvers or in government; his campaigns in the wilderness were conducted in the name of science. He was the New World's first great student of natural history — an explorer and plant collector who established the Colonies' first botanical garden on his farm near Philadelphia.

Bartram's house and the five-acre botanical garden that surrounds it are located on the banks of the Schuylkill River in an industrial section of southwest Philadelphia, engulfed by the city, which was miles away when Bartram and his son William, who also was a famous naturalist, were living. But the unique farmhouse the father built with his own hands and the trees and shrubs associated with both Bartrams are little changed.

John Bartram, a Quaker, was born in Pennsylvania in 1699. A widower with two young sons when he bought his farm in 1728, he began the construction of his field-stone home after his second marriage in 1729. The date of completion is carved in the gable, reading "John–Ann Bartram, 1731." The gable also records, with a distinct diagonal joint, a widening of the house engineered by Bartram as his family and fortune increased. (Ann bore him nine children.) The original home was long and narrow, three rooms on the first floor and three on the second, with an attic above. The kitchen end included a huge chimney and

101

John Bartram, the New World's first great student of natural history, established America's first botanical garden on his farm near Philadelphia, where he had begun the construction of his field-stone house in 1729. Later, to widen the house, a new façade was added on the river side with a recessed porch and three crude Ionic stone columns. Bartram was also an ingenious craftsman; he framed the windows in stone and carved fruits, plants, and classical symbols on the lintels.

The Quaker builder's creed, inscribed below a second-story window: "It is God alone Almighty Lord the Holy One by me Ador'd. John Bartram 1770."

part of the wall from a small house Bartram obtained with his farm. A Swedish settler had built it in 1684.

Bartram followed Pennsylvania custom in building his farm home of stone rather than of brick or frame. The fertile land on the west bank of the Delaware abounds with ledges of soft, easily worked gneiss, and there are valleys where limestone is available to furnish mortar.

His handiwork in stone, however, eventually departed from the simple practices of his neighbors. Bartram enjoyed working with stone, and in the correspondence that has survived him tells a friend how he split huge slabs for his building projects. A watering trough and a cider press he cut in a rock ledge can be seen at the garden. Bartram went all out as a stone carver and designer when he enlarged his home. He widened the house by building a new façade to face toward the river; it was dominated by a recessed central porch framed by three crude Ionic stone columns. The windows in the bays on each side of the porch are framed with carved stone instead of wood. Bartram cut fanciful little medallions depicting fruits, plants, and classical symbols in the lintels. His creed is carved in a large stone below a second-story window. "It is God alone Almighty Lord the Holy One by me Ador'd. John Bartram 1770," he proclaimed.

Bartram also added a room he called his study under a shed roof at the gable end of the house. An ugly frame addition which encloses the upper portion of the riverfront porch probably was made after his death in 1777.

The interior of the house reflects the utilitarian ideas of its Quaker builder. The entrance through a central doorway on the façade away from the river leads into a center hall no deeper than the original structure. The stairs to the second floor, in this cramped area, split near the top and wind both left and right. There are six small bedrooms crowded beneath the attic. Odd little cupboards built into the chimney breast both in the kitchen and in the bedroom above are said to have been used by John Bartram, and by his son William, to protect and dry botanical specimens and seeds.

The house has been furnished with the plain early American pieces a Quaker farmer would have preferred. A few of John Bartram's personal possessions are displayed. A curiosity among them is a small bell he used on his plant-collecting trips. Bartram tied the bell around his horse's neck to help him find his mount when he was afoot in the forest.

Bartram's garden is a city park. The house and garden can be visited any day of the year.

Grumblethorpe, Germantown

The name of this field-stone country home at Germantown, now a part of Philadelphia, was applied in jest by the grandson of the man who built it. Grumblethorpe was "John Wister's big house," beloved and long occupied by his descendants, but not without its problems for those who made it their home.

The exterior of Grumblethorpe and some of the characteristics of the interior are peculiar to the industrious, frugal Germans who established their community on the outskirts of Penn's city. The first colonists settled Germantown for the Frankfort Company in the 1690s. John Wister followed them to Philadelphia from the Rhineland in 1727 and soon made a fortune as a merchant. Wister's "big house" in Germantown, completed in 1744, was the first suburban dwelling erected on that high ground overlooking the city; there, his family could escape the summer heat and fevers associated with Colonial Philadelphia.

The house was much larger and much more elegant than neighboring homes, but the Germantown custom of plastering the interior walls with mixed clay and straw, then whitewashing, was followed. John Wister's grandson, Charles, complained in his memoirs that the flaking coats of whitewash were at least a quarter-inch thick and that the insect population of the walls had reached incredible proportions. He coated them heavily with lime plaster — so heavily that the handsome architraves, or moldings, of the doorways and windows are sunk into the wall instead of projecting beyond the surface.

The fireplaces in both the parlor and the winter kitchen — converted to a dining room when a rear wing was built — are set at an angle in a corner. They were huge caverns, requiring immense quantities of fuel, which Charles rebuilt to their present proportions.

The exterior of Grumblethorpe, which the grandson also altered, has been restored by the Philadelphia Society for the Preservation of Landmarks exactly as John Wister built it. A pent eave projects above the first-floor windows and twin doorways of the street façade, and also around the gable ends and rear of the dwelling. It is interrupted by a small balcony

John Wister made his fortune as a merchant. He built Grumblethorpe in 1774, on high ground, where his family could escape the summer heat. The frugal and industrious nature of the settlers of Germantown is apparent in the house that was once considered the largest and most elegant in what was then a suburb of Philadelphia. The second entrance, a "visitors' door," opens into the parlor. The benches on both sides of the stoops invite all to sit.

above the doorway that leads to the center hall, and there is a similar balcony at the rear. The other entrance from the street is a "visitors' door" which opens directly into the formal parlor. Wooden benches flank the stoops at both entrances, which have divided "Dutch" doors.

Grumblethorpe's invitation to sit and visit on the stoop under the pent eave reflected the hospitality of John Wister. His welcome to friends and distinguished guests was maintained by the family, and the constant procession of visitors may have had more influence than the peculiarities of the house in his grandson Charles's designating it "Grumblethorpe." But one uninvited guest during the Revolution was overtaken by misfortune. The British general James Agnew had requisitioned Grumblethorpe before the Battle of Germantown. He was shot from his horse at the start of the battle and brought back to Grumblethorpe's front parlor. A stain on the floor of that room is said to mark the spot where the general bled to death. John Wister was at his home in the city, where he also was forced to house British soldiers.

John Wister was a member of the Society of Friends and an ardent horticulturist. His garden at Grumblethorpe was well known to the botanists and naturalists of his day and of later years.

Wister's pioneer venture in erecting a country home at Germantown led many Philadelphians to follow suit. They staged a runaway flight to that suburb late in the eighteenth century, leaving only vestiges of the early German community in the subsequent building boom. Philadelphia was the capital city in 1793, when the yellow fever struck and deaths mounted into the thousands. The Congress, like most of the residents who had the means, fled to the hills of Germantown. President Washington spent that summer and fall and part of 1794 in a handsome Georgian mansion not far from Grumblethorpe known as the Deshler-Morris house, now maintained by the National Park Service.

John Wister's "big house" was acquired by the Landmarks Society in 1940. The last member of the family to occupy the house, a great-grandson of the builder, had died thirty years before, and Grumblethorpe was then threatened with demolition. The Society has furnished its rooms to match their bold early Georgian, almost Queen Anne, quality. A few family pieces have been returned to the house. It is open the year round, Sundays excepted.

Samuel Powel — painting attributed to Angelica Kaufman.

Philadelphia's Powel House

Philadelphians, by tradition, entertain at home; the custom was firmly established by wealthy families during the middle years of the eighteenth century.

The town house renowned for lavish dinner parties, receptions, and balls, both before and after the Revolution, belonged to Samuel Powel, who was elected mayor of Philadelphia in 1775 and remained in office until the British occupation of the city in 1776. Unlike his many wealthy Tory friends, he favored liberty for America and was returned to office as mayor when Philadelphia belatedly reorganized its municipal government in 1789.

Every notable visitor to Philadelphia during the nation's founding years visited Number 244 South Third Street to be entertained by Samuel Powel and his wife, the former Elizabeth Willing, whose brother was a partner of Robert Morris, financier of the Revolution. "Dined at Mr. Powel's," wrote John Adams to his wife, Abigail, in 1787, when he was attending the Constitutional Convention at Independence Hall. "A most sinful feast again! Everything which would delight the eye or allure the taste: curds and creams, jellies, sweetmeats of various sorts, twenty sorts of tarts, fools, trifles, floating islands, whipped sillibub, etc." Parties at the Powels' were not forgotten. Sally Franklin, a year earlier, sent word to her father in London that she had danced with General Washington at the Powel home.

The house was built in 1765, not by a Powel but by Charles Stedman, and was then reputed to be the handsomest in the city. It remains the finest of the scores of surviving eighteenth-century brick dwellings along Philadelphia's narrow streets near Independence Hall, in a district known as Society Hill. Its typical row-house façade, embellished by columns

109

Elizabeth W. Powel — by Matthew Pratt.

The Powel house, built by Charles Stedman in 1765 and acquired by Samuel Powel four years later, stands in Philadelphia's Society Hill. It follows the narrow row-house plan typical of Quaker City streets, only hinting at the lavish interiors.

During the Revolutionary years, the cream of American society was entertained in the fashionable Georgian home of the mayor of Philadelphia. The silk brocade draperies in the drawing room are contemporary with the house.

and entablature at a fanlighted doorway, is a deceivingly modest introduction to the elegant rococo architectural detail and decoration within. The rooms reflect the height of Georgian fashion, but for all their formality remain warmly hospitable. Powel, who had inherited his fortune from his grandfather, known as "Samuel Powel, the rich carpenter," acquired the house in 1769, shortly after his marriage. He and his bride filled its rooms with fine furniture, paintings, and sculpture from Europe, where Powel had spent the years 1761 to 1767 in an extended grand tour.

The restoration of the Powel house began in 1931, when Miss Frances Wister organized the Philadelphia Society for the Preservation of Landmarks to save the structure from demolition. It had become a mattress factory. Much of the fine interior woodwork was purchased by the Philadelphia Museum of Art to prevent its destruction. Important sections, notably the arch in the entrance hall and the chimney piece in the dining room, were brought back to their original locations in the house after restoration began. But the woodwork from one second-floor room was sold to the Metropolitan Museum in New York, where it is exhibited as the Philadelphia Room in the museum's American Wing. The

Philadelphia Museum also displays the original upstairs drawing room. The rooms in the house are replicas. The brocade draperies at the windows, however, are contemporary with the house. The material was a gift from Powel's descendants, who had inherited the cloth.

The house is handsomely furnished in the style of the period, but only a few of the treasures the Powels collected have found their way back within its walls. The mahogany knife boxes in the dining room were theirs, and in the same room a few pieces of the Sèvres ware given to the Powels by President and Mrs. Washington are on display.

The house is especially interesting, architecturally, as an illustration of the elegance that can be achieved in row-house design. The row house, which was brought to American cities from London, makes the most of a narrow city lot. The side walls at the front of the house are shared by its neighbors on both sides, though the Powel house today has a garden flanking one wall, the result of the purchase and demolition of a neighboring dwelling. The rear wing of the house, designed as servants' quarters, is narrower and opens at one side to a yard.

The room arrangement in the interior is simply an enlarged and more elaborate version of the typical Philadelphia row house. The doorway opens into an entrance hall that runs the full depth of the front part of the house and contains the stairway to the floors above. Doorways at the side of the hall give access to two rooms on the first floor, and the pattern of hallway and two rooms is repeated on the floors above. The front rooms on the upper floors, however, extend the full width of the house — a circumstance that resulted in the second-floor front room's being frequently used for entertaining. In the Powel house the decoration of this room, the full thirty-foot width of the house, resulted in what was certainly the best known, if not the handsomest, town-house drawing room in America during the first years of the Republic. A visitor who turns the landing at the top of the wide, easy staircase today, and walks into the drawing room can share the pleasure Washington, Jefferson, and other notable guests of the Powels must have experienced when they first saw its splendor. The house is open all year round, except Sundays.

Mount Pleasant

Philadelphia's pride, next to Independence Hall, is Fairmount Park, four thousand acres of green fields and woodland on both banks of the Schuylkill River and along its tributary, the Wissahickon. The terrain is hilly and the heights overlooking the river became the country estates of the wealthy in the eighteenth century. Their mansions were preserved as the city acquired the land, and the finest are open to the public.

The most ornate of the Schuylkill dwellings was built by a swashbuckling, eccentric Scot, Captain John McPherson, on a hilltop he bought in 1761. He made his fortune as a privateer in the West Indies, raiding both French and Spanish shipping from 1757 to 1763, and survived a number of bloody battles. His right arm was shot off early in this hazardous career when a French man-of-war shattered his first command out of Philadelphia, the *Brittania.*

Captain McPherson obviously gave orders that his mansion be, as John Adams later described it, "the most elegant country seat in the Northern Colonies." It is one of the few Georgian dwellings north of Virginia flanked by dependencies symmetrically placed to enhance the grandeur of the central manor. The walls are stuccoed cast stone, scored to imitate ashlar construction which would have required large blocks of masonry. The corners of the house are finished with prominent brick quoins.

The interior of Captain McPherson's mansion makes almost too lavish use of Georgian ornamentation. Fluted pilasters, cornices with dentils, and exquisitely carved scrollwork are everywhere. The pedimented doorways flanking the drawing-room chimney piece are purely decorative, since there is nothing but solid wall behind them. Magnificent furnishings to match this rococo splendor have been placed in the house by the Philadelphia Museum of Art.

During the Revolution the rugged Captain McPherson apparently tired of his isolated life as lord of the manor. One of his sons had been killed in the assault on Quebec in 1775, and the other was with Washington. He had been rebuffed by Congress in his ambitions to

113

Mount Pleasant was built in 1761 by a one-armed Scottish sea captain, John McPherson, who made his fortune through privateering. The house John Adams called "the most elegant country seat in the Northern Colonies" is flanked by formal dependencies and was erected on a hill above the Schuylkill River in what is now Fairmount Park, Philadelphia.

The upstairs hall (*below left*) shows the extreme richness of woodwork and plasterwork. Perfect symmetry is maintained by the false, purely decorative door placed on the left.

build and command a privateer navy. Mount Pleasant, which he had first called Clunie, after his home in Scotland, was offered for sale.

The buyer was General Benedict Arnold, military governor of Philadelphia after its evacuation by the British. Mount Pleasant was Arnold's wedding gift to Peggy Shippen, his second wife, daughter of one of the city's wealthiest aristocrats, but the Arnolds never enjoyed Mount Pleasant's elegance. The purchase was recorded in 1779, when the embittered Arnold had plunged into the graft and lavish living that made him a traitor. The general went off to other commands, ending at West Point in infamy. Mount Pleasant was confiscated by the State of Pennsylvania in 1780. It was leased that year by Baron von Steuben, but he, too, was called away on military service. Von Steuben went South to campaign against Arnold, by then a British brigadier.

The builder of the mansion, Captain McPherson, remained a colorful character in Philadelphia until his death in 1792. He lectured on astronomy and invented a bed he maintained would ward off mosquitoes and all insects, but the one-armed old sea-dog was best known for the city directory he published in 1786. He listed the inhabitants alphabetically and by street number when that information could be obtained. McPherson was frank, though obscure, when the residents refused to cooperate. His directory is full of entries that read "I won't tell you," "cross women," and other phrases to explain the missing names.

Mount Pleasant was owned by Peggy Shippen Arnold's father for a brief period after the Revolution and sold in 1792 to General Jonathan Williams, the first superintendent of West Point. It remained in his family until the middle of the nineteenth century, when it became a beer garden. It was acquired by the city of Philadelphia in 1868. It is open all year except on holidays. Cedar Grove, Woodford, Sweetbriar, and Strawberry Mansion are other notable Fairmount Park houses open most days of the year. Guided tours are available through the Philadelphia Museum of Art.

116

President James Buchanan — detail
of a painting by George P. A. Healy.

Wheatland
in Lancaster

The Lancaster, Pennsylvania, home of the nation's only bachelor President, James Buchanan, has its origin in its name. "The Wheatlands," as it was first known, was erected in
1828 within sight of the golden grain fields of Pennsylvania Dutch farms. The builder was
William Jenkins, a banker who appreciated the agricultural source of his wealth and chose
a site for his country home accordingly. There are no wheat fields near the house today,
however. Banker Jenkins, and President Buchanan after him, were the forerunners of the
industrial and residential expansion that has nibbled away at the farmlands of southeastern
Pennsylvania for more than a century. Their fertile soil was the breadbasket of eighteenth-
and early nineteenth-century America, and Lancaster, founded about 1721, was the principal market place. Wheatland, in a residential district of the city today, was suburban from
the beginning.

Jenkins sold the estate to a Philadelphia lawyer who occupied it as a summer home. Buchanan, who was Pennsylvania's leading Democrat, was Secretary of State when he purchased
Wheatland in 1848. The following year he moved to the big brick mansion, then a mile and
a half outside Lancaster, from a house in town. His attractive niece, Harriet Lane, came to
live with him, acting as his hostess at Wheatland and later in the White House, which he occupied from 1857 to 1861. Harriet was the bright and charming toast of the capital during
the dark days when President Buchanan ineffectually tried to compromise away the Civil
War. Wheatland is filled with pictures and personal possessions that evoke the presence of

Wheatland (*overleaf*) was built in 1828 by William Jenkins in sight of the wheat-
fields that have now been swallowed by the town of Lancaster, Pennsylvania.
Greek Revival in style, it became the country home of James Buchanan in 1848.

the lovely girl who continued to use the house as a summer home for her family many years after inheriting the estate from her uncle. Buchanan died at Wheatland in 1868.

A Lancaster family held Wheatland after Harriet's death until it was acquired by the Junior League of Lancaster nearly thirty years ago. The structure was intact, almost as Buchanan knew it. Much of the furniture he and his niece installed on the first floor had never been removed, and additional family heirlooms have since been returned.

Buchanan's study was the headquarters for his electioneering in 1856. He conducted a "front porch" campaign from his home, which the politicians selected as a rallying point for the Democrats. Wheatland clubs were organized all over the nation. A thirty-one-star American flag on the wall of the study, imprinted with Buchanan's name, is a relic of the campaign and is also a reminder of a time when the flag commanded less respect.

Wheatland was built in the Greek Revival period. The main structure is flanked by three-story, flat-roofed wings. A center hall leads from the front doorway to connect with a reception hall across the rear, where the handsome staircase is located. The floor in the front hall is covered with oilcloth finished in blue and white squares to imitate marble tile. This durable material is an 1845 version of the linoleums and other plastic coverings of modern times. The doors and other woodwork in the important rooms — all cut from pine — are handsomely grained with paint to simulate other woods, following a practice that began in early Georgian houses.

One unusual feature of the house is the access to the third-floor rooms, which were the servants' quarters. The canny banker Jenkins installed three stairways — one to the quarters reserved for women, another to the rooms for single men, and a third to the area occupied by married help.

The grounds at Wheatland have shrunk from the original one hundred and sixty to fewer than five acres, but the ample front lawn, the gardens, and several outbuildings remain and are well maintained. The most entertaining of the outbuildings is the "necessary" — the little brick structure that was always a part of the scene but is seldom mentioned. The restoration at Wheatland has included this building, which was a palace of its kind. It is furnished with five varieties of seats, in kindergarten, grade-school, and adult heights.

Wheatland is open to the public from mid-March until December 1.

New Castle:

Old Dutch
&
Amstel Houses

New Castle on the Delaware is a delightfully preserved, historically significant little town. Its origins are Dutch, but the charming brick homes that cluster around the Old Court House on the Green are thoroughly English. The descendants of the settlers who established New Amstel at this strategic location on the great South River built in the Georgian style after New Amstel became New Castle and a part of William Penn's domain.

One typically Dutch brick house, built in 1687, lasted until eighty years ago. The demolition of its quaint stepped gables and steep tile roof, however, did not eliminate the heritage that persists in Dutch family names and in their contributions to the town where the tiny state of Delaware was born.

A strange little dwelling facing the Green, known as the Old Dutch House, is an example of that heritage. The town records indicate that it may have been built before 1704 by Powell Barens, son of a Dutchman who had been naturalized by William Penn. He inherited the site from his mother and had it surveyed in 1701. The house that Barens, or subsequent owners, eventually completed is as odd and intimate as any to be found in a book of fairy tales. The brick walls of its low first story are topped by a great sweep of roof that projects in a sheltering eave over the front windows and door. The roof in the rear extends down over a shed-type kitchen.

The room arrangement is the same as that in New England's seventeenth-century homes — the front door opens into an entrance "porch," or hall; there are a room to the right, and a room to the left, and a central chimney. The stairs to the attic, however, are not in the hall but wind up behind the chimney from the right-hand room. Both ground-floor rooms have doorways to the kitchen, which has a separate fireplace and chimney.

Though the builder of this tiny house may have been Dutch, the interior is finished in typical English Colonial manner. Powell Barens, incidentally, later Anglicized his name to Paul Barns. The dwelling is within sight of New Castle's oldest house of wor-

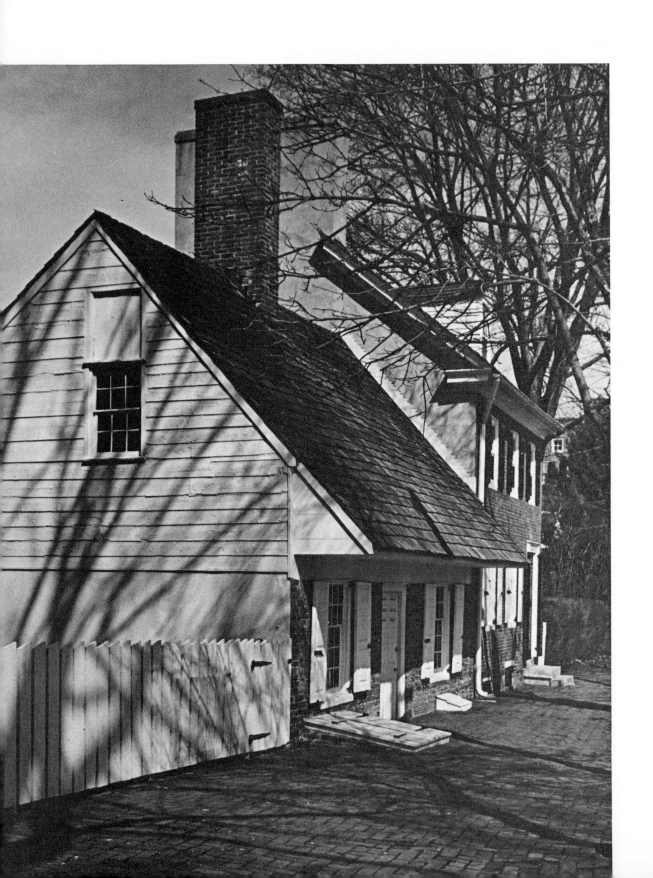

The handsome brick, Georgian-style Amstel House was built in 1730 by Dr. John Finney and later bought by Nicholas Van Dyke, who became president of the State of Delaware.

New Amstel changed to New Castle and Powell Barens to Paul Barns, and the early Dutch heritage so apparent in the house Barens may have built before 1704 gave way to the typical English Colonial influences seen in the interior of his charming little Old Dutch House (left).

ship, Immanuel Church, which was built in 1703. One of the first Anglican rectors is known to have made the Old Dutch House his home.

The New Castle Historical Society maintains the Old Dutch House, which is open from spring until fall. The Society is also owner of Amstel House, open weekdays throughout the year. There is nothing Dutch about this handsome early Georgian mansion except the name, which was the sentimental choice of a twentieth-century owner. The house, however, was at one time occupied by a descendant of a Dutch family, Nicholas Van Dyke, who became president of the State of Delaware in 1783.

Amstel House was built in 1730 by a New Castle physician, Dr. John Finney. He is believed to have added the main portion of the brick dwelling, quite elegantly finished for that period, to an earlier structure which then became the kitchen wing. Van Dyke bought the mansion from Finney. Its big day came in 1784 when Washington was a guest at the reception given by President Van Dyke to celebrate the marriage of his daughter Ann to Kensey Johns, Sr., later the chancellor of Delaware. Portraits of the couple are among the period pieces the Historical Society has assembled to furnish the house.

President Van Dyke's son, Senator Nicholas Van Dyke, built an equally fine house directly across the street in 1799. Twenty-one years later he erected a handsome Federal mansion for his son, Kensey, only a block away. Both are occupied as homes today, which is the happy fate of scores of New Castle's old dwellings.

The three Van Dyke homes reflect the changing architectural tastes within one family over the period of a century. The contrast is most marked in the interiors, which can be seen at least once a year, on New Castle Day, when as many as thirty of the town's privately owned historic houses are opened to the public. That date, for forty years, has been the third Saturday in May.

IV

TIDEWATER
TO BLUE RIDGE
TO FLORIDA

Charleston, South Carolina, 1739.

IV

TIDEWATER
TO BLUE RIDGE
TO FLORIDA

The Tidewater in Virginia — and Maryland, too — is the country that has access to the many navigable rivers that flow into Chesapeake Bay. This world of waterways extends south from the borders of Pennsylvania and Delaware almost to the North Carolina line. Here Englishmen established their first successful colony at Jamestown in 1607. And here the architectural heritage of the plantation society they created can be enjoyed today.

The Tidewater crop that established a way of life for the South was tobacco, for which the planters found a market within sight of their slave-tilled fields. Ships cruised the Chesapeake rivers with goods from England and replaced them with hogsheads of tobacco for the return voyage across the Atlantic.

Towns were slow to develop in country where trade centered at individual plantation docks. Elegant Williamsburg was created as a seat of government to replace Jamestown, not for commerce. Annapolis languished until it, too, became a Colonial capital. The busy port cities did not develop until late in the eighteenth century when the country west of the Tidewater began to funnel crops to shipping points.

The big plantations evolved during the first century of settlement. Only a few of the earlier small homes, such as the medieval brick Adam Thoroughgood House on the Lynnhaven River at Norfolk, now survive. Mount Vernon and Stratford Hall on the upper Potomac and the huge mansions strung out along the James River represent the affluence attained by the second and third generations of the most successful and highly placed families.

The builders of the plantation homes, like most gentlemen of the period, were familiar with architectural design. Some of them employed professional help, however. Richard Taliaferro was mentioned as "our most skillful architect" by Thomas Lee in 1749. Taliaferro was especially active in and around Williamsburg. He built the Wythe house there and may have designed Carter's Grove, the 1750 plantation recently acquired by Colonial Williamsburg. John Ariss, who studied architecture in England, designed many later Georgian houses in Virginia and is believed, by some, to have aided Washington at Mount Vernon.

The way of life that evolved in the Tidewater in time spread west across the Piedmont toward the Blue Ridge, where Thomas Jefferson perched Monticello on a mountaintop overlooking the Old Dominion. Ports such as Alexandria and Annapolis, by the time of the Revolution, were ornamented with town houses where merchants, planters and office-holders gathered for the winter social seasons. The fine mansions that survive, such as the Hammond-Harwood house in Annapolis, served this purpose.

Many leaders of young America came from the plantations. Four of the first five Presidents were Virginians, and three more occupied the White House before 1850. Most of their homes still stand and are open as museums. The dwellings of other Virginians and Marylanders who helped mold the nation, now privately owned, can be visited during Virginia's annual Garden Week in April or during the May House and Garden Pilgrimage in Maryland. Both events help support the restoration of historic homes and the gardens that surround them.

South of the Chesapeake the Tidewater was less hospitable to settlement. The disasters that wiped out Sir Walter Raleigh's colonies on Roanoke Island in the sixteenth century were a foretaste of difficulties to come. Hatteras's barrier islands and the shallow waters behind them barred the ocean-going ships in the tobacco trade. Most of North Carolina remained a region of frontier farming through the eighteenth century, and the palace of Governor Tryon at New Bern was almost an insult in its magnificence.

Rice and then indigo supported another rich plantation world south of Cape Fear. Charleston was the trade and cultural center — and also a bastion against the Spanish from Saint Augustine in the early years. The picturesque, crowded little streets near East Battery and extending to the Old Market reflect the area that was walled against assault from the last of the seventeenth century until 1720 or later. Neither the walls nor any of the houses built before 1730 remain, but the street pattern where the surviving Georgian and Adam and Greek Revival homes were built never changed.

Savannah became the outpost of English settlement in the eighteenth century — an extension of the rice empire that threatened Spain's foothold on the continent at Saint Augustine and eventually inundated Florida with British and then American adventurers. The Georgia city's years of wealth and challenge to Charleston did not come until after the Revolution.

The settlement of the South Atlantic states was substantially complete when cotton began to fill the uplands early in the nineteenth century and the age of steam arrived. The houses described on subsequent pages take the story only to that time, from Maryland to Florida.

130

William Buckland with plans of the Hammond-Harwood house — painting by Charles Willson Peale.

Hammond-Harwood House

It is difficult to identify the designer of a home built before the Revolution. Wealthy men usually dabbled in architecture, accumulating ideas from books and from houses they visited, often abroad. They frequently prepared crude floor plans and elevations for a new home. But the all-important details of construction — the composition of skillfully chosen parts into a completed structure — were left to a joiner, or master carpenter. His taste in selecting and adapting the components and embellishments from the books in his own or perhaps the owner's library usually determined the appearance of the finished building. Most of these eighteenth-century craftsmen are unknown. A few, however, achieved the reputation of architects and are survived by work that can be clearly identified. Such men as Peter Harrison of Newport are known by the public buildings they designed.

William Buckland, however, came to America from England to work on houses. Colonel George Mason brought him to the northern neck of Virginia in 1755 as an indentured servant, to ornament the interior of his new home, Gunston Hall, with woodwork in the latest London fashion. Buckland launched out on his own when Gunston Hall was completed and reached the peak of his career from 1770 to 1774 in Annapolis. The finest Georgian mansions in Maryland's handsome little capital are believed to be his work.

His masterpiece, and final undertaking, was the Hammond-Harwood house. There is no question about the identity of the architect. Charles Willson Peale painted Buckland seated at a table, pen in hand, with an architectural drawing before him. The plan is for Mathias Hammond's house in Annapolis. A copy of this portrait can be seen in the house

131

In 1774 Mathias Hammond, a young lawyer who derived his wealth from fifty-four tobacco plantations, commissioned William Buckland to design the Hammond-Harwood house in Annapolis. This fine Georgian mansion is considered Buckland's masterpiece and shows his passion for academic symmetry. The doorway at the center of a modest exterior is of the type most admired in Georgian architecture.

The most interesting rooms, architecturally, are the large dining room (*left*) on the first floor overlooking the garden and the ballroom (*far right*) above it. A detail of a bedroom is seen at right.

today, replacing the original, which is now part of the fabulous Garvan collection at Yale University.

Hammond was the fourth generation of a distinguished Maryland family. His great-grandfather had been appointed a commissioner to lay out the town of Annapolis. The Colonial capital, in Mathias's day, was the hub of a wealthy society based on the tobacco trade. Mathias inherited more than twoscore plantations. He was just twenty-six in 1774 when work began on the magnificent town house Buckland had designed for him.

The mansion is only two stories high, flanked by wings on either side. Hammond is thought to have agreed to this height, after first considering a three-story house, to avoid obstructing the view of the harbor for Colonel Edward Lloyd, who was finishing the three-story home he had bought from Samuel Chase just across the lane that today is Maryland Avenue. Buckland is also credited with the final design of this home.

Neither Buckland, the designer, nor Hammond, the owner, ever enjoyed the beauty he created. Buckland died late in 1774, at the age of forty. Young Mathias Hammond, as his mansion neared completion, is said to have gone to Philadelphia to buy furniture to complete the home he planned as a wedding gift. His bride-to-be, in his absence, eloped with another man. Up to that point Hammond had been prominent in the affairs of Annapolis, active in the militia and as a buyer of supplies for Maryland's Revolutionary Council of Safety. Suddenly, in 1776, his name disappears from all records. He never occupied the house and left no trace of his activities thereafter. His death was recorded in 1786.

Mathias's house was rented, and after his death went to a nephew, who sold it in 1810. Judge Jeremiah Townley Chase bought the Hammond house a year later, and from him the mansion passed to his daughter, Frances, who married Richard Loockerman. Their daughter, Hester Ann, inherited the house. Her husband was William Harwood, a great-grandson of William Buckland.

The return of a descendant of the designer to his magnificent and well-preserved house occurred shortly before the Civil War. William Harwood brought Peale portraits of his great-grandparents, John and Sarah Buckland Callahan, with him. The rolled-up canvases were found in the attic nearly forty years ago and sold with the contents of the mansion to settle the estate of William Harwood's last surviving daughter.

The house was saved for posterity by Saint John's College, which purchased other fine Annapolis landmarks in the 1920s. The college sold the property to the Hammond-Harwood Association after its formation in 1940. The house is open throughout the year.

James Madison — detail of an engraving from the original painting by Chappel.

The Octagon

Some buildings, like people, seem destined for good fortune. Born with charm and personality, they accept the triumphs and survive the disasters of a busy life to reach a gracious, colorful old age. The Octagon, national shrine and home of the American Institute of Architects at New York Avenue and Eighteenth Street in Washington, fits this description. It was one of the first Federal-period homes built in the national capital — a pioneering venture by one of President Washington's wealthy friends — and also served as Presidential mansion after the British burned the White House in the War of 1812.

The District of Columbia had little more than French Major Pierre Charles L'Enfant's plan to recommend it when Colonel John Tayloe, of Mount Airy, Virginia, decided in 1797 that he would have a town house in Washington. The Octagon's good fortune began with Colonel Tayloe's choice of architect. He turned to one of the geniuses of the age, an eccentric gentleman who had taken a degree in medicine but devoted his energies to architecture, invention, race horses, city planning, painting, writing — in fact, almost everything except the serious pursuit of the profession he had learned in his youth. He was Dr. William Thornton, also famed for his prize-winning design of our Capitol building and for many years first director of the Patent Office.

Thornton's genius, confronted with the problem of placing a home in the narrow V formed by the intersection of one of Major L'Enfant's diagonal boulevards with a cross street, found a solution in the unconventional shape of the Octagon. The doctor curved the front wall of the house, forming a half-circle in the street-corner apex of the V; and this, to

Dolley Madison.

The Treaty of Ghent was ratified in what is today called the Treaty Room on the second floor, above the entrance. Madison used it as his study.

the Tayloes at least, must have given the illusion of an eight-sided home. They called it the Octagon from the beginning, and in later years protested the use of any other name, though the house actually has six sides and not the eight its name implies. The unusual floor plan combines circular and rectangular rooms. Thornton continued the curve within the house to create a distinctive circular entrance hall on the first floor and the handsome Treaty Room above. He also built secret doors, closets, and a hidden staircase in the leftover space between the inner walls and completed the Octagon's mysteries with a tunnel that takes off from the basement in the general direction of the Potomac River.

The Madisons occupied the Octagon early in September 1814, only a few days after the British, having sacked Washington, returned to their fleet in Chesapeake Bay. Thornton, as usual, had a hand in everything. He was the man who found Colonel Tayloe's son Benjamin, and negotiated a lease for the President (the Octagon was not in use by the family at that time of the year); he rode alone into Washington and talked the British out of burning Blodgett's Hotel, which housed his Patent Office; and he helped engineer a safe-conduct for Francis Scott Key aboard a British man-of-war — a trip that resulted in "The Star Spangled Banner."

136

Dr. William Thornton designed the Octagon for John Tayloe in 1797. The unusual house has six sides, circular and rectangular rooms, secret doors, staircases, and a tunnel thought to have led to the Potomac. One of the first Federal-period houses built in the nation's capital, it witnessed many exciting moments when the Madisons moved in after the burning of the White House in 1812.

The French ambassador had resided temporarily in the Octagon at Mrs. Tayloe's invitation when the enemy marched on the capital. His flag saved it from destruction. "French John" Sioussat, the White House steward, must have had a premonition that he would lord it over the Octagon kitchens for a year. He rushed Mrs. Madison's poll parrot from the White House to the French minister's cook for safekeeping while Dolley herself fled to Virginia with a handful of personal belongings and the rolled Gilbert Stuart canvas of George Washington, hastily cut from its frame. Little else was saved from the President's house, which did not become known as the White House until it was rebuilt and white-coated to hide the fire-blackened walls.

The Madisons were quickly at home in the well-furnished Octagon. The President established his study in the circular room on the second floor. Dolley, who loved to entertain, revived her wardrobe with a shipment of Paris gowns, the duty on which, she records, was two thousand dollars. Her dress for the New Year's Day reception at the Octagon, in 1815, was described as "a robe of rose-colored satin, trimmed with ermine, with gold chains and clasps around her waist and arms, and a white satin turban upon her head, whence sprang a tiara of white ostrich plumes."

The big day at the Octagon, and undoubtedly the best party of all, occurred February 17, 1815, when the Treaty of Ghent was received and ratified. The small leather-bound trunk in which Henry Carroll, Henry Clay's secretary, brought the treaty from Europe still rests on Madison's circular table, which occupies the middle of this room today, just where it is thought to have been then. Word of the British defeat at New Orleans had come only a few days before. The celebration began, as Paul Jennings, Madison's valet, remembered it, when Miss Sally Coles, daughter of the President's secretary, opened the curved, paneled door in the great hall and called down the concealed back stairs, "Peace! Peace!" Drinks were ordered for all the servants, and Jennings maintained that Sioussat was drunk for two days — but apparently not until French John and Jennings and Sukey, who was Jennings' wife and Dolley's maid, and the rest of the staff had seen the President and his Cabinet through a mammoth impromptu reception.

Restoration of the Octagon, which had sunk to tenement use, began in 1897, when the architects decided to move their headquarters from New York to Washington. The Octagon was first leased and then purchased from the Tayloe heirs in 1902 for thirty thousand dollars. It is open to the public throughout the year.

Mount Vernon

Washington was first in many things, and architecture is among them. He introduced a design that became a traditional part of plantation homes in America. Mount Vernon was the first country mansion to be ornamented with a piazza two stories high to give the structure dignity and at the same time provide shelter from the Southern sun.

The plan for Mount Vernon's piazza facing the Potomac was part of Washington's final enlargement of his home. The "Great house" that is visited by hundreds of thousands today was not much more than a third its present size in his youth. It was a modest farmhouse, only a story and a half high, with four small rooms on the first floor, known as the Hunting Creek Plantation. Augustine Washington, George's father, is thought to have built it after buying the plantation from his sister. The Washingtons moved into the house in 1735, when George was three years old.

Lawrence Washington, an older half brother to George, changed the name of the estate to Mount Vernon when he made it his residence in 1743, after Augustine died. The name honored British Admiral Edward Vernon, with whom Lawrence had served in the Caribbean. Mount Vernon came into the possession of George Washington in 1754, two years after the death of Lawrence, when he purchased his sister-in-law's life interest in the estate.

The first enlargement of the house began soon afterward. Washington's correspondence with his neighbor, William Fairfax, speaks of the purchase of tools, hardware, and other items abroad. The interior was rearranged and redecorated and the roof raised to provide a full second story and an attic above. Washington was absent on military duty much of the time, and Fairfax guided the work. Colonel Washington's younger brother, John Augustine, managed the plantation.

Washington returned to Mount Vernon in 1758 and the following year brought the widow Martha Dandridge Custis to the renovated mansion as his wife. He had retired from active military service and had fifteen years of life as a country gentleman ahead of him. The

Detail of Thomas P. Rossiter's painting of Lafayette's visit to Mount Vernon.

Augustine Washington, George's father, is thought to have built the first portion of Mount Vernon about 1735. George Washington took possession of the house in 1754 and later more than doubled its size. Although Washington seems to have been his own designer and builder, some historians believe that the architect John Ariss helped the first President with his remodelings.

140

dwelling at Mount Vernon in those years was all that portion which extends from chimney to chimney. Washington's diary records that it was linked to four dependencies by "pallisades" atop brick walls.

Toward the end of these peaceful years Washington began to plan the huge estate he would not have a chance to enjoy, except for brief interludes, until his retirement from the Presidency in 1797. The plantation had grown and prospered, and the Mount Vernon he had in mind was to be the headquarters for five farms. The buildings near the mansion once housed nearly one hundred people and provided clothing and supplies for a larger number on the outlying farms.

Washington the engineer, farmer, and executive was quite capable of acting as architect, as well. Architectural historians have conjectured that John Ariss, a Virginian who studied in England to become a professional architect, may have had a hand in both remodelings of the mansion — but have found no proof. Washington's papers record the ordering of materials from England in 1773, and the following year he wrote to a friend: "I am very much engaged in raising one of the additions to my house, which I think (perhaps it is fancy) goes on better whilst I am present than in my absence."

That addition was the library and his bedroom above at the south end of the house. The other addition, on the north, was the banquet hall, which is two stories high. The piazza that frames the entire length of the riverfront façade with eight tall columns was to be Washington's finishing touch.

The major work, like the first remodeling many years before, was completed in Washington's absence. Lund Washington, a relative, acted as manager of the plantation during the Revolution, and the general kept in touch with him by letter during the war years. "The chimney of the new room should be exactly in the middle of it," were his instructions for the new banquet hall. The interior of that room was not finished until Washington had once again retired from military service, before his first term as President. The painting of the banquet hall, the paving of the piazza with flagstone imported from England, and the installation of the weathervane on the cupola in 1787 marked the completion of the mansion as it is today.

The step-by-step growth of the hospitable residence that Washington once called "a well resorted tavern" can be readily traced on the west façade. Georgian design called for a balanced arrangement of all the parts of a structure. This Washington never could achieve after the first remodeling. The construction of the stairs in the wide center hall required a variation in the size of the rooms on either side, and an off-center placement of the outside door. Washington "balanced" the later additions to Mount Vernon by adding false windows above the banquet hall.

The plantation that was the first President's creation might have been lost without the vision of Miss Pamela Cunningham and her Mount Vernon Ladies' Association, formed 111 years ago. Neither state nor Federal governments were interested in financing its preservation. Mount Vernon is open every day.

142

"The Marriage of Nellie Custis at Mount Vernon took place on the last birthday of her foster father, George Washington. She is shown kissing him as her husband watches. The couple went to live at Woodlawn.

Woodlawn

The landmarks associated with George Washington, so dramatically summed up in the magnificence of Mount Vernon, come to a conclusion at nearby Woodlawn Plantation. The first President never saw the mansion at Woodlawn, but he selected the site and gave the land — approximately two hundred acres of the Mount Vernon lands west of Washington's home — to his foster daughter, Eleanor Parke Custis, and his favorite nephew, Major Lawrence Lewis, as a wedding gift. It included the Dogue Run farm and a grist mill that still stands on the banks of the little stream. The highest point, Gray's Hill, overlooked the little valley and the Potomac far beyond, with the cupola and chimneys of Mount Vernon in view. "Few better sites for a house than Gray's hill . . . are to be found in this country or elsewhere," the General told the Lewises.

The couple was married at Mount Vernon on Washington's last birthday, February 22, 1799. The ceremony took place "about candlelight," Washington recorded in his diary. Both of the young people lived with him at Mount Vernon, and continued to reside there until 1802, when Martha Washington died and they moved to partially completed Woodlawn.

The portrait of Eleanor Parke Custis Lewis, made
about the time of her marriage, is supposedly a
copy of a painting by Gilbert Stuart.

Dr. William Thornton designed Woodlawn in the
tradition of the great Georgian plantation homes,
employing delicate Adamesque detail in the Federal style. The house was built in 1802, within sight
of Mount Vernon, for Major Lawrence Lewis and
his bride, Eleanor Parke Custis.

144

They had chosen Dr. William Thornton, the talented amateur who had won the competition for design of the Capitol, as their architect. He was a friend of the family and responsible for two of the finest town houses in Washington — the Octagon and Tudor Place.

Thornton planned Woodlawn in the tradition of the great Georgian plantation homes that the first families of Virginia had been building for a century. The main structure is balanced by connecting "hyphens" to wings, and beyond them there are flanking dependencies. The stately center hall contains a curving staircase and has wide double doors at both ends. The front doors open on a small porch beneath a portico facing toward Mount Vernon. Visitors, however, circle the house and enter from the gardens in the rear.

Woodlawn marked the end of an era. Architecturally, Thornton's use of delicate, Adamesque detail is in the Federal spirit. Economically, the land needed to support an establishment of the magnitude of Woodlawn was no longer easy to acquire in the Tidewater. And the world the Lewises had shared with the Washingtons had vanished. Only distant Mount Vernon remained in view from their hilltop to remind them of what had been.

Their life at Woodlawn, however, was "on a grand and liberal scale," as one visitor noted in 1817. The furnishings that have been returned to the restored mansion belonged for the most part to the family and recall their interests and such events as the visit, in 1824, of the Marquis de Lafayette. The Lewises' son Lorenzo inherited Woodlawn at the death of his father and sold the plantation in 1846 to a group of Quakers from Philadelphia. The house, which had been vacant for a number of years, became the headquarters for a real estate operation that forecast the doom of big estates. Woodlawn Plantation was subdivided into small farms by the Quakers; the purchasers included former slaves.

The mansion was eventually deserted and almost in ruins shortly before 1900. A new owner, the playwright Paul Kester, restored Woodlawn and at that time changed the wings to their present appearance by increasing their height and adding dormer windows. Miss Elizabeth M. Sharpe was the next owner and sold it to Senator and Mrs. Oscar W. Underwood of Alabama. The mansion was purchased by the Woodlawn Public Foundation in 1948, and title was transferred to the National Trust for Historic Preservation in 1957. Woodlawn is open throughout the year.

Gunston Hall

Of all the riverside plantations open to the public in Virginia the relatively modest home of George and Ann Mason, Gunston Hall, is one of the most pleasantly situated. Mount Vernon, in keeping with the majestic stature of Washington, boldly commands a view of the broad Potomac, while Gunston Hall, like the man who built it, is more retiring in its outlook over the same river. The house sits peaceful and secure, facing out across its famous ancient boxwood garden to a little valley that opens on the water.

Mason's plantation adjoined the Washington holdings. Gunston Hall and Mount Vernon are less than five miles apart, and the owners and their families frequently visited each other, either by water or by the much longer route overland. Mason recorded that he returned by carriage from Mount Vernon one day with a gift of jasmine and rose plants, and his letters speak of cider and a side of venison, "the first we have killed this season," going to Washington.

George Mason, born in 1725, was the elder statesman among the Virginians who played leading roles in the birth of the United States. Patrick Henry, Richard Henry Lee, and Thomas Jefferson were often entertained at Gunston Hall while they consulted with their wise and modest host. Mason was offered public office many times, but refused it, preferring to contribute his services in other ways. He wrote Virginia's first constitution and the state's famous Bill of Rights, which first declared "That all men are created equally free and independent and have certain inherent natural rights ... the enjoyment of life and liberty ... and pursuing and obtaining happiness and safety."

Mason began the construction of Gunston Hall in 1755, just one hundred years after his great-grandfather's first land patent had been recorded in the colony. That first Mason, also named George, had left England for America after an uprising in which he had opposed the king, and the great-grandson, despite the wealth he had accumulated as a planter, was just as outspoken and independent. Mason was a Virginia delegate at the Philadelphia

George Mason, by Boudet after Hesselius.

Gunston Hall was constructed between 1755 and 1758 in Lorton, Virginia, for George and Ann Mason. The story-and-a-half modest brick house reflects a seventeenth-century simplicity. The plan is believed to have been Mason's, but William Buckland was brought from England to do the carving and joining — the beginning of his outstanding architectural career in America. The unique five-sided river porch is Mason's design; it overlooks the magnificent box gardens of Gunston Hall.

The elaborate carving made the Palladian drawing room a Buckland masterpiece. The painting of Ann Eilback Mason is by D. W. Boudet, after Gustavus Hesselius.

Convention of 1787 at which the Constitution was adopted, but he refused to sign the document, declaring that it allowed the continued importation of slaves and that the rights of individuals were denied protection — an omission the first ten amendments, the Bill of Rights, sought to correct four years later.

Gunston Hall, completed in 1758, gave William Buckland his start in America, and Buckland left within it some of the finest woodwork of the mid-Georgian period. The plan for the story-and-a-half house is believed to have been Mason's. He asked his brother Thomson, then studying law in London, to find a carpenter and joiner for the building. Thomson selected William Buckland, who agreed to work out his passage to America at Gunston Hall. Buckland, the successful architect who later sat for a portrait by Peale at Annapolis, spent three years on the job.

The Chinese Chippendale dining room he created for Mason was the first of its kind in the Colonies and the equal of any that survive. The drawing room, Palladian in motif, is almost too elaborately decorated with the exquisite carvings Buckland employed to embellish cabinets, windows, and doors. Here he obviously sought to impress on a scale that all but overwhelmed with its magnificence.

The drawing room and a ground-floor bedroom across the center hall are both on the south side of the house, facing toward the boxwood gardens and the Potomac. The doorway that opens to this view from the hall is sheltered by a delightful little porch which George Mason devised in "the latest fashion" with Gothic arches. The porch on the other side of the house has a classical pediment, patterned after a Greek temple but interrupted by a central arch. The entranceways are almost the only ornamentation on the exterior of Gunston Hall.

The mansion at one time had two dependencies on the north. These buildings were lost during Gunston Hall's years of indifferent ownership after the Civil War. The house was given to the State of Virginia by its last owner, Mr. Louis Hertle of Chicago, as a shrine to be administered through the National Society of the Colonial Dames. The restoration was begun in 1951. Gunston Hall is open throughout the year, except Christmas Day.

Thomas Jefferson — detail of a painting by Rembrandt Peale, 1805.

Monticello

There is magic in Thomas Jefferson's remarkable home, perhaps because he built it on a mountaintop, close to the sky. There is no other explanation for its escape from destruction late in the Revolution when the British general, Banastre Tarleton, and his raiders rode into Charlottesville, hoping to capture the owner of Monticello, who then was Governor of Virginia. "Bloody" Tarleton's men stormed up to the mansion, but only the servants were there. Jefferson had barely had time enough to gather up his most valuable papers and slip off to join his wife in a safe place. The troopers, much to the amazement of the staff at Monticello, did not pillage the house. Their orders were capture of the owner and not destruction of the building, they said.

The home Tarleton spared was Jefferson's avocation all his adult life. Classical, rambling Monticello, the plantation complete in one structure, was his creation from its four-hundred-foot long foundations to the ingenious weather vane above the portico. He was the architect, the building foreman, and the landscape designer.

The construction of Monticello, from the grading of the site to its completion in its present form, extended over forty-one years. Jefferson inherited the estate from his father in 1757 and twelve years later began clearing and leveling three acres on the hilltop above Charlottesville. The first portion to be built was the little brick pavilion at the end of the southwest terrace walk; after the burning of Jefferson's boyhood home, Shadwell, he completed what is now called Honeymoon Cottage as bachelor quarters, which became a temporary home for his bride, Martha Wayles Skelton, a widow whom he married in 1772. The wedding took place on New Year's Day, and the Jeffersons reached their building project on the mountaintop in a blizzard.

The never-ending construction and improvement of Monticello must have complicated Martha Jefferson's life. The mansion in its first form was completed about 1782. The Marquis de Chastellux, a visitor during the Revolution, described it then as "one square pavil-

151

Thomas Jefferson was the architect and landscape designer at Monticello for much of his life. His unusual one-structure plantation home overlooking Charlottesville and the University of Virginia from a mountaintop was first "completed" in 1782, but did not assume its finished classical form until well into the nineteenth century. The "sky room" replaced the library under Monticello's prominent dome between 1796 and 1809.

Jefferson's famous alcove bed with its crimson cover stood halfway between his study and his bedroom.

ion, the entrance of which is by two porticoes, ornamented with pillars. The ground floor consists of one very large lofty saloon . . . above it is a library of the same size; two small wings, with only a ground floor and attic story, are joined to this pavilion, and communicate with the kitchen, offices, etc., which will form a kind of basement story, over which runs a terrace."

Jefferson's early plans for his house called for porticoes two stories high, rather than their present one-story height. He changed the structure between 1796 and 1809, replacing the upstairs library with the chamber he called his "sky room" under Monticello's prominent dome. At this time he also completed the other components of his novel all-in-one plantation — the dependencies under the long flanking terraces, all connected by a covered passageway.

The inventiveness of the President who was an architect is delightfully evident at Monticello. Jefferson's designs include a weather vane that can be read without looking up to the sky; a dumb-waiter direct to his wine cellar; a revolving door with shelves for serving; and his famous bed halfway between his library and bedroom. His architectural tastes were ahead of his time. The Capitol at Richmond, which he designed in 1785, anticipated the Classic Revival by a generation. Monticello was finished in the same spirit.

Jefferson is thought to have first suggested the architectural connection of the plantation dependencies and mansion at Brandon, one of the James River estates, built in the 1760s by his friend, Nathaniel Harrison. The James Semple house at Williamsburg is also credited to Jefferson, who at one time had ambitious plans (happily thwarted by their cost) to convert the Governor's Palace at the Virginia capital into a Greek temple.

The joy of the retired President and champion of individual freedom was the construction of the University of Virginia at Charlottesville. He not only initiated the project and designed the buildings but even staked out their location. Every step of construction came under his eye, aided by a telescope from his perch at Monticello when he was unable to take time for a visit to the valley below.

Thomas Jefferson, who was born in 1743, died at Monticello July 4, 1826, the fiftieth anniversary of the Declaration he had written. He is buried in a family graveyard on the edge of the mountain only a few feet from his home. The title to the graveyard was all that remained for his daughter after his death. His estate had to be sold to satisfy the debts that had accumulated through his lavish hospitality at Monticello, where he also served as "friendly adviser, lawyer, physician and even gardener of his vicinity," in the words of one visitor in 1817.

Monticello was purchased in 1923 by the Thomas Jefferson Memorial Foundation from the Levy family, who had owned it since before the Civil War. The mansion and the gardens are as Jefferson knew them — faithfully following the plans and directions found in his papers. The estate is open every day.

Stratford Hall

Stratford Hall, the ancestral home of the Lees of Virginia, is quite as remarkable as the famous family this monumental mansion once housed. The big H-shaped brick dwelling, topped by its boldly clustered chimneys, is an awesome monument to the generations of wealth and responsible leadership that produced Robert E. Lee. The hero of the Confederacy, the man who turned down the command of the Union Army because he "could take no part in the invasion of the Southern States," was born in Stratford Hall in 1807. His was the fourth generation to live in the mansion his great-grandfather's brother had built in the years 1725 to 1730.

The builder was Thomas Lee, the venturesome scion of one of the Old Colony's most prominent families. His grandfather, Richard Lee, had come to Virginia in 1641, patented many tracts of land, and held important offices at Jamestown, then the Colonial capital. Richard Lee II, Thomas's father, was a member of His Majesty's Council, an office that became traditional in the family until the Revolution.

Thomas Lee, who served as Governor of Virginia, was a giant among the planter aristocrats whose ships swelled the trade between England and America. He built Stratford above the cliffs of the lower Potomac to replace his boyhood home, which was destroyed by fire. The loss prompted Queen Caroline, wife of George II, to contribute a bounty of three hundred pounds toward the construction of the new manor, heart of a plantation that covered sixteen thousand acres.

Lee, who was then in his thirties, built the house and outbuildings of brick burned in kilns at the site. The principal dependencies are symmetrically located at the four corners of Stratford. They include Lee's one-story office and the kitchen. Both these small buildings are on the south side, which is the approach to the mansion. Their clipped gable ends produced a quaint "jerkin-head" roof, a hold-over from medieval times.

There is an Old World, almost forbidding austerity in the great mass of Stratford Hall,

155

Thomas Lee, builder of Stratford Hall.

The great Southern Civil War general and statesman Robert E. Lee lived at Stratford as a child.

Thomas Lee, great-granduncle of Robert E. Lee, built Stratford Hall in Westmoreland County, Virginia, between 1725 and 1730. It was designed in the old Tudor H-shape with great clustered chimneys, each supporting a platform from which the plantation owner viewed the Potomac and approaching ships. The house has a raised basement; the main floor begins ten feet above ground. The apparent severity of the structure is softened by the variety of color and texture in the brick. Centrally placed, the drawing room (*left*) has doors that open to the river and land sides of the house. The ancestral home of the Lees reflects the wealth, good taste, and intellectual integrity of the long line of famous Americans who occupied it.

which is unlike any other mansion that survives from early Georgian America. Lee's H-shaped plan gave him twenty rooms on the two floors of the house — sixteen with corner exposures. He embellished the interior with paneling, dadoes, and other woodwork then fashionable in London. The great hall on the second floor, terminus of the prominently balustraded steps that rise on the exterior of the house, is magnificently finished with panels and pilasters rising to the high dome of an "inverted tray" ceiling. A catwalk in the attic above connects the two chimney clusters, where stairs lead to the crow's-nest platforms from which Lee watched his ships.

Thomas and Hannah Ludwell Lee raised a notable family in the great house. Two of their sons, Richard Henry and Francis Lightfoot Lee, were signers of the Declaration of Independence. The eldest, Philip Ludwell, and their daughter, Hannah, were born while Stratford was under construction. Philip inherited the plantation. His sister defied convention to become Virginia's foremost Colonial champion of women's rights.

Hannah married Gawen Corbin, of neighboring Peckatone, who died when she was still quite young. He willed her Peckatone provided she did not marry again. Hannah had already asserted her independence by leaving the established Anglican Church to become a Baptist. She rebelled against the conditions of the inheritance, which saddled her, alone, with a huge plantation in a world where men made all the rules. She fell in love with a Dr. Richard L. Hall and invited him to live with her at Peckatone. Hannah had two children by Dr. Hall in this "marriage," which was accepted by the community and lasted until his death. She was buried with him a few years later.

It was Philip Ludwell Lee's daughter Matilda who married her cousin, Henry "Light-Horse Harry" Lee, and became the mistress of Stratford late in the eighteenth century. The brilliant Colonel Lee, three times Governor of Virginia, was one of Washington's favorite young officers. He was serving in Congress at the time of Washington's death and eulogized his chief as "First in war, first in peace, and first in the hearts of his countrymen" — words that have stirred generations of Americans. Matilda Lee died before she was thirty, and Henry Lee later married Ann Hill Carter, from Shirley Plantation on the James River. Robert E. Lee was their third son.

Robert Edward Lee lived at Stratford only as an infant. The Lees moved to their town house in Alexandria when he was four. The "mother's room" where he was born had been renovated in the lighter Federal style by his father. A graceful Adam mantel and matching woodwork in the room have been preserved by the Robert E. Lee Memorial Foundation in the restoration of Stratford Hall. The property was acquired by the Foundation in 1929, from Charles Stuart, who was related to the Lees by marriage. The purchase included eleven hundred acres of the original plantation, to which subsequent additions have been made. The restoration of the mansion, outbuildings, gardens, and the surrounding fields and woods closely approximates the huge establishment Thomas Lee, with the help of Queen Caroline, long ago carved out of the wilderness along the Potomac. Stratford Hall is open the year round.

158

Adam Thoroughgood
House

A stay in Williamsburg, to sample the pleasures of the sophisticated little city that was Virginia's capital in the eighteenth century, usually leads to Jamestown, where the conquest of the wilderness began only one hundred years earlier. The site of the first settlement soon became the capital of a province with thousands of inhabitants. Who brought them to the New World?

A small brick house east of Norfolk holds the answer. The Adam Thoroughgood house on the west bank of the Lynnhaven River, which survives as a reminder of the venturesome young men who helped populate Virginia, commemorates Captain Adam Thoroughgood's success in this endeavor. It was built in the heart of a ten-square-mile grant of land given to the captain in 1635 by the Governor and Council of Virginia for bringing one hundred and five persons to settle in the colony.

Captain Thoroughgood was a minister's son. He was just seventeen when he shipped away to Virginia, under an indenture, in 1621, but he soon became listed as a "gentleman" residing at Hampton and in 1629 and 1630 was a Burgess in the Assembly at Jamestown. Thoroughgood returned to England and married fifteen-year-old Sarah Offley. They are believed to have built their home on the Lynnhaven in 1636, though there are no records to confirm the date. The architect H. Chandlee Forman thinks the house was built by the captain's son Adam, who died in 1685, but it could even have been the work of a grandson by the same name.

Whoever the builder may have been, the construction conforms to the medieval practices the colonists brought to America and adapted to their needs during the earliest years. The tall T-shaped chimneys at each gable end of the forty-five-foot-long house represent the heating arrangement that was preferred in the brick houses of the south, instead of the massive central chimneys of Massachusetts. The chimney at the west end of the Thoroughgood house is an impressive pyramid built outside the wall — an arrangement that per-

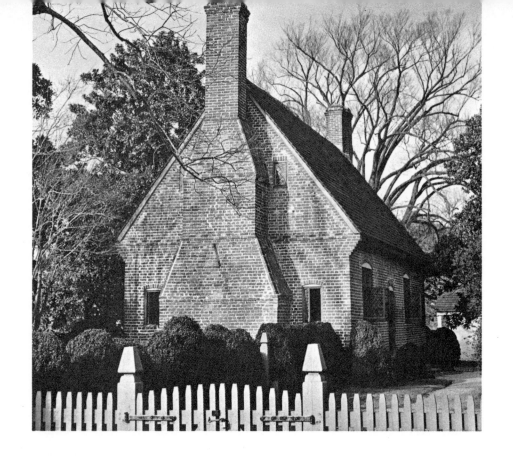

Adam Thoroughgood arrived in America as an indentured servant but had become a man of position by 1636, when he is thought to have built his house near Norfolk. The archetype of the small seventeenth-century Virginian farmhouse, it reveals the strength and simplicity of building practices brought by the colonists from England. It is solid brick, has a steeply pitched roof covering the usual four rooms — two of them in the attic, with small windows in the gables — and tall T-shaped chimneys at each gable, which provide the desired heat. The molding around the living room fireplace (*left*) is an eighteenth-century addition. The kitchen window (*right*), with its casement sash and rectangular panes, looks out over the garden leading to the river.

sisted for two centuries in the prominent "fiddle" chimneys of farmhouses in the upper South. The steeply pitched roof covers the usual four rooms of a small medieval dwelling — two attic rooms, with fireplaces and tiny gable windows, and two rooms on the first floor with a passage, or hall, between them. A door at the rear of the passageway opens toward the river — a New World innovation that became standard practice in Southern homes, where center halls with both front and rear doors insure cool breezes during the summer months.

The Thoroughgood doorways and windows alike on the ground floor are topped by the flat, segmental arches employed by bricklayers in the seventeenth century. The brick walls facing the river and on the gable ends are laid in alternating courses of headers (the end face of a brick laid crosswise to the wall) and stretchers (the long face of a brick laid lengthwise), known as English bond. The front of the house, on the land side, was given a more decorative and costly finish. Here the bricks are laid in Flemish bond, in which the headers and stretchers alternate in each row.

The Adam Thoroughgood house, in common with many architectural landmarks, has undergone several restorations. The careful research that determined the location and size of the original windows and corrected earlier attempts to give the home of the Thoroughgoods eighteenth-century airs has brought it close to its original appearance. The most marked difference, perhaps, exists in the roof. Its precipitous slopes today are covered with fireproof tiles that imitate shingles. The original roof was fashioned of oak clapboards, which can be seen from a vantage point inside the attic.

The interior of the Thoroughgood house is furnished simply with early antiques. One ground-floor room, the parlor, has been kept in its eighteenth-century "modernization," in which the fireplace was narrowed, the chimney breast paneled, and a dado and box cornice added around the room. The Georgian staircase in the passageway between the front and back doors apparently replaced an earlier "winder" at this time.

The house and its attractive garden are owned by the city of Norfolk and administered by the Norfolk Museum of Arts and Sciences. It is open from the first of April until November.

Tryon Palace

The construction of Tryon Palace at New Bern, North Carolina, was one of history's magnificent miscalculations. Britain's Royal Governor William Tryon's taste was excellent, but his timing was atrocious. He chose a coastal location for the capital of a society destined to flower inland after the Revolution, and almost immediately saddled his province with building costs the struggling citizens could not afford.

Tryon had made up his mind, when he was appointed Royal Governor in 1765, that the first permanent capital of North Carolina should be established at the colony's largest town, New Bern, where the Trent River joins the Neuse estuary flowing into Pamlico Sound. The port was midway between Virginia and South Carolina, the wealthier, more accessible provinces that had given birth to North Carolina.

Swiss colonists had formed a company to establish the town under the English flag in 1710, naming it for their home community. Though Indian raids had led to the abandonment of the Swiss project after its first three years, descendants of the original settlers remained at the time of William Tryon's first visit in 1764.

Tryon brought John Hawks, a "master builder," with him from London to design and build his palace. Artisans were imported from England and from Pennsylvania to work on the huge central house and flanking wings, all built of brick manufactured at New Bern. The project was far enough along in 1770 for the governor, his wife, and their nine-year-old daughter to move into their new home. The Governor's Council and Provincial Assembly met jointly at the palace in December of that year.

The Crown didn't give Tryon much time to relax in the splendor he had created — splendor that had no equal, the revolutionist Francisco Miranda declared, "even in South America, a land of palaces." Tryon was sent to New York as Royal Governor in 1771. The man who succeeded him, Governor Josiah Martin, publicly deplored the great expense of the palace — it cost seventy-five thousand dollars — and the tax burden it had created. But

Abner Nash, second governor of the independent state of North Carolina, served in 1780 and 1781, during the Revolutionary War period.

Tryon Palace was designed and constructed in 1764 at New Bern, North Carolina, by John Hawks. The handsome and richly decorated palace was commissioned by Britain's Royal Governor William Tryon and became the first Capitol of North Carolina. It consisted of a huge central house and two wings. The majestic entrance hall is in the classical style.

Martin also made additions, which included a smokehouse, poultry house, and a dovecote.

British occupancy of the palace ended in May 1775. Governor Martin took refuge from the gathering Revolutionists on a British naval vessel off Cape Fear, while his family sailed away to New York.

The palace became the first Capitol of the state of North Carolina in 1777, and four governors were inaugurated in its assembly room. But Tarheel leaders were not at ease in the architectural grandeur a British governor had created in the tidelands. They were finding their destiny in the Piedmont uplands to the west. Washington visited New Bern in 1791 and recorded in his diary: "Dined with the Citizens . . . and went to a dancing assembly in the evening; both of which was at what they call the Pallace, formerly the Government House and a good brick building but now hastening to Ruins."

The last State Assembly met at Tryon Palace in 1794, the year the capital was moved to Raleigh. Barren rooms, once filled with the fine furnishings of the Tryons and the Martins, were then rented to lodgers, and a variety of tenants occupied the Council Chamber and other ground-floor quarters. The ruin Washington had noted became complete when a spectacular night fire gutted the main building in 1798; the east wing was later demolished.

That might have been the last of Tryon Palace. The town in time extended a street across the site, and new homes were built where gardens and dependencies had bordered the Trent River. But the west wing survived, though strangely altered, and the architectural magnificence of North Carolina's vanished first Capitol became a legend in New Bern.

The legend was brought to life by a woman who was a native of New Bern, though she and her wealthy husband lived in the prosperous Piedmont, at Greensboro. Mrs. James Edwin Latham's millions enabled the state, through a specially created Tryon Palace Commission, to regain its Colonial Capitol as it appeared before the Revolution. Materials were brought from England to match Hawks's drawings and fragments excavated on the site. An inventory of Governor Tryon's possessions, prepared after a fire loss in New York, guided the furnishing and decoration of the interior.

The palace is open throughout the year, except Mondays.

Charleston:

Manigault House
&
Russell House

The confluence of the Ashley and the Cooper Rivers does not, as Charlestonians like to believe, form the Atlantic Ocean. But the V at the mouth of the rivers does provide them with a special world apart — a world that makes better use of its architectural heritage than any community in America.

Few of the old homes in Charleston are museums. They are for the most part the residences of a society that enjoys contemporary life in an environment inherited from the past. The trickle of restoration that began nearly fifty years ago has become a major source of the city's present vitality; a renaissance, as it were, that could not have happened anywhere else. Charleston is a proud and stubborn little city that was stopped dead in its tracks by the war it launched in 1861. A way of life and wealth was gone. The mansions that had been built in the eighteenth century and the first half of the nineteenth were all that remained. They were safe from demolition because no one wanted city land, and they waited, often in slum use, for the first artists and writers to discover them shortly after World War I.

There are no survivals in Charleston of seventeenth-century dwellings, but the names of the men from the British Isles, the West Indies, France, and the northern colonies who settled there between 1670 and 1700 are perpetuated in the homes their descendants built. One of them, the Joseph Manigault house at 351 Meeting Street, was designed by the owner's brother, Gabriel, the owner of many plantations and a talented architect as well.

Gabriel and Joseph were great-grandsons of Pierre Manigault, a Huguenot who fled from religious persecution in France. Their grandfather Gabriel was regarded as the richest man in South Carolina in the early Provincial years. His namesake Gabriel was sent abroad at the start of the Revolution to study law at Geneva and in London. He returned to Charleston and took the oath of allegiance to the Crown when the British captured the city in 1780.

The house Gabriel Manigault designed for his brother is believed to represent his first

The Nathaniel Russell house (*opposite page*), one of the most beautiful of the Adam period, was designed in 1809 by Russell Warren. The "flying" staircase (*above*), with its light and graceful curving lines, is an outstanding feature. The painting of Nathaniel Russell (*above right*) was made by Edward Savage about 1787.

Gabriel Manigault, who designed his brother Joseph's Charleston house (*below*) in 1790, was the first to introduce the grandeur and sophistication of the Federal style. It has the new polygonal and oval form, gray brick, and curving bays projecting on three sides of the mansion. The two-story piazzas are typical of Charleston.

project as an architect. It dates from 1790 and is built in the Adam style. The walls are a gray brick much used in Charleston. Curving bays project on three sides of the mansion. One, at the rear, encloses a magnificent unsupported circular staircase. The projection on the east was Manigault's concession to the tastes and climate of Charleston — a two-story piazza. Another utilitarian piazza ornaments the front façade.

The Joseph Manigault house passed from the family and was saved from demolition by Charleston's pioneer preservationists more than a generation ago. It was later bought for taxes by Princess Pignatelli and given to the Charleston Museum. The present furnishings match the restrained elegance of the Adam mantels, doorways, ceilings, and cornices, and include many pieces associated with the Manigaults. The house is open throughout the year.

169

The Charleston Museum also maintains a Georgian town house, open all year, that was President Washington's residence when he visited the city in 1791. This was the dwelling of Thomas Heyward, signer of the Declaration of Independence, built by his father, Daniel, in 1770. The President did not dislodge Heyward during his week-long stay. His host was not living in town but at his rice plantation, a move that was almost a ritual for the wealthy families when hot weather arrived and yellow fever stalked the town.

The Heyward mansion is on Church Street, in the architecturally entrancing area near the Battery where the Lords Proprietors staked out the original settlement. Charlestonians refer to it as a "double house," a term applied to the center-hall design that was popular throughout the Colonies. The "single house," however, is peculiar to Charleston. These homes are built with the gable end facing the street and a two-story piazza extending along the side. Entrance from the street is through a doorway leading to the piazza, thence to a stair hall in the middle of the house, which has single rooms on each side of the stairs, front and rear.

The "single house" is designed for cross ventilation and is credited to the West Indian planters who migrated to Charleston. It became an almost universal design throughout the city. None of the many that survive, unfortunately, is open to the public except for the two weeks in early spring when tours of private homes are arranged by the Historic Charleston Foundation. The house Thomas Legare built in 1760, almost directly across Church Street from the Heyward mansion, is an outstanding example of the type.

The Foundation, which is the backbone of Charleston's restoration of old houses, has its headquarters in the Nathaniel Russell house on Meeting Street, one of the nation's most beautiful homes of the Adam period. Two elliptical rooms and a circular "flying" staircase make the interior unusual. It was built about 1809 for Russell, a native of Rhode Island who made his fortune as a merchant in Charleston. The design is thought to be the work of another man from Rhode Island, architect Russell Warren. The house is open all year.

Symbol of Savannah:

Owens-Thomas House

Savannah, Georgia, is a Colonial city, founded in 1733, but only a handful of the fine old homes that line the tree-shaded streets date back to the eighteenth century. The majestic elegance of the later Classic Revival, symbol of wealth in ante-bellum days, predominates in the old city.

The few surviving eighteenth-century buildings are of limited architectural interest, for in its early years James Oglethorpe's border settlement was more concerned with hostile Spaniards and Indians than with structural elegance. The town also suffered from disastrous fires. Davenport House, the handsomest Georgian dwelling, now the headquarters of Historic Savannah, Inc., is an architectural anachronism; it was built in 1820.

Owens-Thomas House, completed a year earlier, was nearly as far ahead of its time in America as the Davenport house was out-of-date. Greek and Roman architectural form and detail began in Savannah at this great and gracious mansion on Abercorn Street, facing Oglethorpe Square; it set the pace for the environment that persists in Old Savannah to this day.

The design of the Owens-Thomas house is pure Regency, transplanted from England at the time when the architect John Nash, that "very great master, who found us all brick and left us all plaster," was reworking the face of London with classical buildings. William Jay, a brilliant young man who had been caught up in this architectural revolution, drew up the plans in London in 1816 and came to Savannah the following year to superintend the construction that had already begun.

The son of a prominent Nonconformist clergyman, Jay was clever, witty, and just twenty-one when he landed in Savannah to build the house commissioned by Richard Richardson. (Both Richardson and Jay's sister had married into Savannah's Bolton family.) Jay designed a number of superb homes in Savannah and in Charleston, South Carolina, during a brief seven years in America, but seems never to have worked as an architect afterward.

171

The Owens-Thomas house began the Classic Revival in Savannah, Georgia. It was built by William Jay in 1819 for merchant Richard Richardson, and is pure Regency in style. The delightful balcony on the south side of the house (*above*) has four supports shaped like acanthus leaves. From it General Lafayette addressed the people in 1825.

He found an ideal site in the lot facing Oglethorpe Square, in a city full of ideal sites for town houses, thanks to the street plan adopted by founder Oglethorpe. His surveyor followed the familiar gridiron pattern when the town was laid out but assigned more land to the frequent criss-cross streets and public squares than to lots for private use. The Owens-Thomas house fills one of these lots, one that fronts on a public square, has ample room for a garden and outbuildings at the rear, and is bordered by a street on each side. This happy situation is repeated all through the old city, about two square miles in size. The latticework of streets, interrupted every few blocks by parklike public squares, is well adapted to the motorized twentieth century. There are through streets for people in a hurry, but also plenty of space for a pleasant mingling of pedestrians, motorists, trees, and gardens.

Jay adapted what he had learned in England to American materials. The walls of the Owens-Thomas house are of tabby — a mixture of oyster shells, lime, and sand often used in the southeast; they are faced with stuccoed brick on the interior. Stone was brought from England for cornices, pilasters, and other decorations. Most delightful, and most photographed, is the balcony on the south side of the house, which has four supports shaped like acanthus leaves. Another similar balcony was planned for the same side but eliminated from Jay's design when the ship carrying stone and metal was lost at sea.

Jay's subtle, restrained use of classical forms to create attractive living space reached perfection in the salon of the Owens-Thomas house. This is the first room to the right as you enter from the double-curved portico that faces Oglethorpe Square. The ceiling is ornamented with circular molding in Greek fret pattern, curved to descend slightly at the corners, where delicate moldings from the fretwork are gathered as if they were folds of drapery. The square room, in effect, expands beneath this illusory dome.

Like the salon, the drawing room across the entrance hall has a pair of large windows facing Oglethorpe Square. The long north wall of this room, however, is broken only by a niche, topped by a narrow, horizontal aperture of Greek key design, lighted from the outdoors. Jay used yellow glass here to give the illusion of sunshine from the north light.

The house is elegantly furnished in the period before 1830. Many of its furnishings were willed with the structure to the Telfair Academy of Arts and Sciences by Miss Margaret Gray Thomas in 1951. She had inherited the property from her grandfather, George W. Owens, who bought the house in 1830 from the Bank of the United States. Richardson, the original owner, occupied his home for only one year; financial troubles forced him to deed it to the bank in 1820. The house is maintained as a museum by the Telfair Academy; it is closed during the month of September.

Saint Augustine:

"The Oldest House"
&
Arrivas House

They call it "The Oldest House" in Saint Augustine, Florida. It may be, even though the house is about one hundred and fifty years younger than the town, which was the site of North America's first permanent white settlement in 1565. None of the palm-thatched huts that housed Spaniards in the sixteenth and seventeenth centuries have survived. Substantial homes such as The Oldest House were not built until the Spanish governors had finished construction of Saint Augustine's Castillo de San Marcos, now administered by the National Park Service. This fort, often besieged but never conquered, is built of coquina, a shell rock quarried from an island that shelters Saint Augustine from the open sea.

The townspeople of Saint Augustine did not get rock for building with until about 1710. The thick coquina walls that enclose part of the first story of The Oldest House were erected between that date and 1723, when Tomás Gonzalez Hernandez, fusilier to the king of Spain, and his wife Francesca are recorded as living there.

This earliest house, as presented by the Saint Augustine Historical Society, approximates its appearance in 1790, after three families — two Spanish and one British — had lived in it. Oldest House, like all the ancient dwellings along Saint Augustine's quaint, narrow streets, exhibits a mixture of architectural influences — Spanish, primarily, but overlaid with British and American ideas. The clapboard second story and wood shingle hip roof were added to The Oldest House when Britain held Florida from 1763 to 1783. Hernandez had raised his family many years earlier in a one-story house, perhaps one-third the size of the present structure. It probably had a thatched roof. Heat was provided by charcoal in a brazier, or *brasero*. Food was cooked there, too — although Tomás, as his family grew, may have built an outdoor hearth for Francesca not much different from the barbecue pits found in back yards today. A more substantial but typical Spanish courtyard kitchen can be seen on The Oldest House grounds today.

Hernandez was in his sixties when England, having driven France from North America, concluded a treaty with Spain that gave her East Florida. Hernandez and his neighbors fled to Havana, leaving their homes to be sold by an agent when British buyers could be found. The Oldest House was not sold until 1775, to Major Joseph Peavett. He enlarged the house to approximately its present size, adding the second story, the fireplace and chimney, and the typically British double-hung, glazed windows with outside shutters.

Britain returned East Florida to Spain at the end of the Revolution, and The Oldest House soon had another Spanish owner. Peavett died in 1786, and his widow, Mary, married a fast-living young man less than a month after his death. Her new husband ran through her fortune, insulted the Spanish authorities, and was banished from Saint Augustine. The house was seized for debt in 1790 and sold to Gerónimo Alvarez, who became the city's most successful baker.

Oldest House, as Alvarez' home, played a leading role in Spain's brief experiment with constitutional government early in the nineteenth century. Saint Augustine's town council, or *cabildo,* often met there when the royal governor, who had no sympathy with democratic processes, barred the members from government premises. Alvarez was mayor, or *alcade.* He was responsible for the monument to constitutional government under Spanish rule that still stands in Saint Augustine's Public Plaza. Alvarez, unlike Hernandez, remained in Saint Augustine when Spanish rule ended. The Americans, migrating from Georgia and the Carolinas, had all but taken over the city by the time Spain sold Florida to the United States. The new republic attracted Alvarez and his son Antonio, who was given the house in 1839. Antonio, like his father, became mayor of the city and held other offices as a prominent citizen of the United States.

The senior Alvarez probably added the porch on the east and the second-story rooms on the north or courtyard side of the house. The porch might have been added to provide the family with a substitute for the similar second-floor galleries, Spanish in conception, that project over the street from many Saint Augustine homes. As an American, on the other hand, Alvarez no doubt grew accustomed to the front door Major Peavett had cut into the street wall of the house. The older custom was a side, courtyard gateway from the street. The only openings on the first-floor, street façade of a Spanish house were windows, without glass but screened with gratings or latticework. The *reja,* a latticed window that projected out beyond the wall and gave a half-hidden *señorita* an opportunity to see both up and down the street, was much used.

The furnishings in The Oldest House are those that such a prosperous, well-established family as the Alvarezes might acquire. Most of the bedroom furniture on the second floor (including delightful, delicate furnishings in a child's room) are from the collection assembled abroad by Isabel Ross, on loan from the Buffalo, New York, Historical Museum. The Ross items also include examples of Spanish glass and tile, exhibited in a museum that adjoins The Oldest House and is headquarters for the Saint Augustine Historical Society.

The Museum's graphic portrayal of Saint Augustine's colorful past contributes help-

"The Oldest House" in Saint Augustine, Florida, was built between 1710 and 1723. Tomás Gonzales Hernandez, fusilier to the king of Spain, is recorded to have lived there first. The house had achieved its present appearance by 1790 through a mixture of Spanish, English, and American owners and influences. It was briefly used for meetings of the Saint Augustine town council in the early nineteenth century.

177

The restored Arrivas House, now a museum, is Spanish in design and construction. It utilizes oyster-shell "tabby" for thick walls. The house and grounds were restored by the Saint Augustine Historical Restoration and Preservation Commission to illustrate building practices in eighteenth-century Florida.

ful background to an appreciation of the house and should be visited first. A tour of the Arrivas House, restored by the Saint Augustine Historical Restoration and Preservation Commission is suggested for architectural *aficionados* interested in the restoration of America's oldest city to the appearance it had when it was Spain's last outpost in North America.

The Oldest House is open every day.

178

V

THE MISSISSIPPI
VALLEY

(*Preceding page*) Saint Louis, Missouri, 1846.

THE MISSISSIPPI VALLEY

The land rush into the Midwest was one of the world's great migrations to fertile new land. It began with the log-cabin builders who crossed the Appalachians after the Revolution and continued for more than half a century until lonely sod houses began to dot the Great Plains.

The American and foreign-born homesteaders, however, were not the original pioneers. The French had penetrated the heartland from Canada during the seventeenth century and claimed the mid-continent until the eighteenth century was two-thirds gone. Fur-trading *voyageurs* and farmer *habitants* from Canada had settled on the banks of the Mississippi while the English were still clearing forests along the Atlantic Coast. La Salle's lieutenant, Henri de Tonti, had launched a sailing ship on the Great Lakes to ferry furs from Wisconsin to the Saint Lawrence before William Penn founded Philadelphia. The town of Kaskaskia, later engulfed by the shifting Mississippi, was established in southern Illinois in 1695. French control of the big river was complete by 1714 after the Sieur de Bienville, the founder of New Orleans, had fortified Gulf-country settlements from Mobile to Natchez.

France lost her North American empire after the fall of Quebec in 1763, but the *habitant* families remained. Their Creole world, now under the flag of Spain, became a haven for the exiled Acadians from Nova Scotia, who found a Gallic homeland in the bayous of Louisiana.

The architectural ideas that the French brought from Canada and from the West Indies have influenced generations of home builders in the Gulf country. The roofed-over *galeries* that take the place of interior hallways and serve for the location of stairs evolved from simple Norman cottage designs. The first step was to surround the hall-less cottage with the galleries. The "raised cottage" followed, when the wood structure was raised on brick or other durable supports to escape rot and flooding and stairs had to be built. Though

183

none of the earliest seventeenth-century French homes has survived man and nature, similar eighteenth-century houses exist along the Gulf and also on the upper Mississippi.

The Norman, and French-Canadian, house has a steep hipped roof. The *habitants* in the Illinois and Louisiana country added galleries for shade and protection from rain. The roof then was extended by giving the lower part a flaring, flatter pitch. Two old French houses of this type have been restored as museums in the Saint Louis area.

The Cahokia Courthouse in East Saint Louis, Illinois, dates from about 1737. Originally the home of a French family, it was used as a courthouse and jail prior to its first restoration, when it was moved to the Saint Louis Fair grounds in 1904. The old house then was erected in Grant Park, Chicago, and returned to Cahokia just before World War II.

The Bolduc house in Saint Genevieve, Missouri (see page 203) is part of a French community that was built directly across the Mississippi from old Kaskaskia, Illinois. Many houses in this town show their eighteenth-century heritage despite alterations.

Far south, near the Gulf, the most readily accessible eighteenth-century French cottage houses are the misnamed Old Spanish Fort in Pascagoula, Mississippi, Madame John's Legacy in New Orleans' French Quarter (see page 185) and Connelly's Tavern in Natchez (see page 193). The last is an interesting and handsome contrast to the stately ante-bellum mansions for which Natchez is famed.

A monumental, porticoed dwelling was the mark of success in the period from 1820 to 1850. Wealth came quickly to the planters, merchants, and bankers in the fertile heartland. Their big homes are the outstanding architectural heritage of the mid-continent east of the Mississippi, from the Lakes to the Gulf. The old Georgian style is evident in only a few early houses, mostly in the valley of the Ohio. Adena, near Chillicothe (see page 219), echoes earlier design brought from the East.

The classical influence dominated in the Midwest, producing notably handsome homes at its inception during the Federal period. The Taft Museum in Cincinnati (see page 213) and Rosalie at Natchez (see page 193) both profit from the restrained use of classical elements in contrast to the extravagant ornamentation of some later Greek Revival mansions. The white-painted wood walls of the Taft Museum, incidentally, are typical of northern Ohio, rather than the Ohio River region. Many dignified white-frame Federal-period homes survive the New Englanders who developed the Lake Erie country.

The first American settlers in the Midwest followed the waterways, as the French had before them. The Mississippi and its navigable tributaries were the source of commerce. Wealth and power were concentrated near its banks until the railways gave the inland towns their opportunities as well.

The homes described in the following pages are all related to people who pioneered along the big river. Even those built in early Victorian times — the Campbell house in Saint Louis and the Villa Louis at Prairie du Chien (see page 207) — were the homes of men who had made their fortunes in the early river trade that won the North American heartland for the United States.

184

The Baroness Micaela Pontalba.

Vieux Carré:
Pontalba Apartments & Madame John's Legacy

They call it the French Quarter, but the architecture of the Vieux Carré, or Old Square, in New Orleans is best described as Creole. Louisiana's Creoles are Americans of French and also of Spanish descent. It was their adaptation of Old World culture to life in the New that produced the gallery-lined little streets, the hidden courtyards, and the landmark buildings that surround what was first the Place d'Armes, then the Plaza de Armas, and finally Jackson Square.

Nearly all of the Quarter was built after 1788, when the first of two disastrous fires swept the area. The years of greatest prosperity and rebuilding followed the Louisiana Purchase, when New Orleans was freed of all foreign restraint in serving the booming Midwest. The climax for the Vieux Carré came in 1849, when the Baroness Micaela Pontalba began the construction of the impressive dwellings that bear her name and line two sides of Jackson Square.

Micaela was the red-haired, strong-willed daughter of Don Andres Almonester, one of the city's wealthiest men, and his Creole wife. The Palais Royal in Paris was her inspiration for the Pontalba apartments facing the Square to complete the grand design her father had helped initiate in the 1790s. Don Andres at that time took the lead in the building of the Cabildo, the Cathedral of Saint Louis and the Presbytery. Micaela consulted several architects, the famous James Gallier, Jr., among them, in the design of the Pontalba buildings, but apparently dominated the work herself. She designed the ironwork displaying her initials which encloses the second-floor galleries, and had it fabricated in New York. She personally supervised the construction, clad in trousers to facilitate climbing through the unfinished buildings.

The Louisiana State Museum, which owns the Lower Pontalba buildings, has furnished one of the dwellings much as one of the well-to-do Creole families who first occupied it would have done. The décor is Late Empire, which Louis Philippe called "French Antique"

185

The Palais Royal in Paris inspired the red-headed Baroness Micaela Pontalba to construct the apartments (*right*) that line two sides of Jackson Square (*left*) in New Orleans. She consulted the famous architect James Gallier but supervised the construction herself and designed the ironwork that bears her initials.

Jean Pascal, a sea captain, probably built the first version of this typical Louisiana-French house (*below*) in New Orleans about 1728. The Madame John for whom it is named was his widow. Spanish Governor Manuel de Lanzos, the owner, rebuilt the house above a lower story of brick after fire swept New Orleans in 1788.

and from which the English derived Victorian. This was the period in which the New Orleans cabinetmakers Prudent Mallard and François Seignouret made their reputations, and their work is well represented.

The Museum also maintains on Dumaine Street, not far north of the Square, one of the rare houses in the Quarter that are typical of the homes built in New Orleans early in the eighteenth century. It is Madame John's Legacy. She was the widow of Jean Pascal, the master of a French galley who died in the Indian attack on Fort Rosalie at Natchez in 1729. Her legacy was the house Jean had built on a lot he received from La Compagnie des Indies in 1722, the year New Orleans became the capital of French Louisiana.

The original Legacy was not at the present site. The building that survives apparently was moved in 1783 by Renaldo Beluche. Manuel de Lanzos, later the Spanish Governor of Mobile, bought the old house, which was badly damaged in the 1788 fire. After it burned Lanzos commissioned Roberto Jones, a carpenter, to salvage what he could and to erect a similar home on a lower story of brick. Doors, hardware, and a number of beams apparently were usable.

What Lanzos got is a typical Louisiana French "raised cottage" with a distinctively flared, double-pitch hipped roof. These cottage homes with roofs that sweep down over galleries were first built with vertical logs set in the ground. The wood structures were later set on low stone foundations to protect them from rot and eventually raised on a lower story of brick in low-lying areas like New Orleans. The entrance stairs to the Legacy are in the rear gallery, facing brick slave quarters and outbuildings across a narrow court. The close quarters in the city prevented the addition of galleries at the ends of the dwelling in addition to those front and rear. The old French cottages in less crowded surroundings customarily are ringed by galleries on all four sides.

The Pontalba restoration and Madame John's Legacy are open throughout the year, except Mondays. Only the lower floor of the latter can be visited, however, until the State Museum undertakes long-postponed repairs of the upper rooms.

The Shadows-on-the-Teche

The National Trust for Historic Preservation describes the architecture of the Shadows-on-the-Teche, at New Iberia, Louisiana, as "a brilliant example of foreign influences that culminated in the distinctive house style of the Louisiana country." The house style, of course, is plantation ante-bellum, and the foreign influences are largely French.

The Shadows, however, is much more than an architectural monument to a way of life. It was the ancestral home of a brilliant, fun-loving bachelor who married a house. The man was Weeks Hall, and his consuming passion for thirty-five years was the mansion and garden his great-grandparents built on the banks of the Bayou Teche.

David Weeks, the owner of four sugar plantations near New Iberia, was the builder. His wealth had come from the land grants his father, William, obtained from the Spanish governors of Louisiana in the last years of the eighteenth century. The Shadows was David Weeks's town house for his family, centrally located in the village on the Teche. He bought four and a half *arpents* (roughly the equivalent of four acres) on the south bank of the navigable bayou that winds through the Evangeline country just north of the Gulf and hired James Bedell, a master builder, to erect his mansion. The work began in 1831. The walls are of pink brick, burned from local clay. Weeks and Bedell built two-story-high galleries, both front and rear, supporting the front roof above the gallery on eight Tuscan columns. The rear gallery does not extend across the full width of the house, being flanked by bricked-in wings on both sides.

Access to the second-story rooms is by outside staircases at the corners of the gallery, in the Creole manner. The stairs are shielded by louvered shutters. The principal, central chamber on the ground floor is the dining room, which was served from a kitchen dependency. The drawing room is directly above, on the second floor. All rooms are reached from the galleries at both levels instead of from interior halls.

David Weeks enjoyed his house for only four days after its completion in 1834. He

189

David Weeks, wealthy sugar-plantation owner, commissioned James Bedell to erect the Shadows-on-the-Teche in 1831. It saw the gay and gracious life of the South until the Civil War. The house was occupied by Union forces and after the war suffered decades of neglect. Weeks Hall, the great-grandson of the builder, devoted thirty-six years of his life and fortune to caring for the house, which became his home in 1922, and its gardens. A fun-loving bachelor, he entertained many prominent artists and writers. The dining room (*above*) looks toward the garden and the Bayou Teche.

traveled north to New Haven, in ill health, hoping the change of climate would prove beneficial, and died shortly after arriving in Connecticut. His widow raised their six children and managed the plantations with the help of her brothers until 1841, when she married Judge John Moore.

When Weeks Hall, the great-grandson of David, returned to the Shadows after World War I, the mansion was dilapidated, the dependencies in ruins, and the once exquisite

Weeks Hall and his English setter "Lady Shadow's Ghost," otherwise known as "Spot."

garden a jungle. Hard times had come to the Shadows with the Civil War. Mrs. Moore died in a bedroom on the attic floor of the house while it was occupied below by Federal officers. Various members of the family in later years tried to keep up the mansion without lasting success.

Weeks Hall resolved to restore the gardens under the century-old live oaks along the Bayou Teche and to preserve the house and its contents for posterity. He had studied in America and abroad to be an artist and was well known as a critic. All of his income now went to the improvement of the Shadows and to the entertainment of his friends, who included many prominent artists, writers, and actors. At his death in 1958 Hall willed the Shadows to the National Trust along with his estate as endowment for its upkeep. The family papers and the furnishings of five generations within the mansion were included in his bequest. The Trust, aided by the Hall endowment, has returned the Shadows to its era of greatest brilliance, when it was the home of the Weekses and the Moores. The house is open throughout the year.

NATCHEZ:

Rosalie
&
Connelly's Tavern

The story of Natchez begins at the site of Rosalie, one of the handsomest of the famous ante-bellum mansions in that Mississippi town. Rosalie was the name Bienville gave to the fort he established in 1716 to hold this strategic location for France; he chose it to honor Rosalie, Comtesse de Pontchartrain. Here is the most southerly point at which the high ground of mid-America is accessible to the big river that continues through endless bottom-lands to the distant Gulf.

Wealthy Peter Little perpetuated the name of the old fort one hundred and four years later when he commissioned his brother-in-law, James Griffin, to design and build his home on part of the land on which the troops of France, Great Britain, Spain, and eventually the United States had been garrisoned. Little, who had made his fortune in real estate, married his ward, Eliza Low, and installed her in the big brick Federal-period mansion, surrounded by gardens that then reached to the high bluff overlooking the river. Several acres of the garden enclosed by a brick wall are still maintained by the Mississippi Society of the D.A.R., which owns the house.

Little sent Eliza to Baltimore schools for her education after their marriage. She became deeply religious and some years later established Rosalie as a luxurious haven for visiting ministers. The constant procession of clergy drove Little from his home. He resolved the quarrel by building a guest house for Eliza's friends within sight of Rosalie; it came to be known as The Parsonage, and the Littles eventually deeded it to the Methodist Episcopal Church.

The Parsonage is one of the homes open during the Natchez Pilgrimage festival in March, when nearly twoscore ante-bellum mansions may be visited. About a dozen, including Rosalie, are open throughout the year.

The furnishings at Rosalie and the decoration of the interior are of a later period than the house. It was sold in 1856, after Peter Little's death, to Mr. and Mrs. Andrew L. Wilson.

They renovated the interior but faithfully preserved the Federal exterior, which is dominated by a pedimented portico shielding fanlighted doorways to both the first- and second-floor center halls. The Wilsons' furniture was bought in New York in 1857 and 1858, and its Victorian magnificence fills the house today, since Rosalie never left the Wilson family until its purchase by the D.A.R. in 1938.

Mrs. Wilson was a Confederate patriot who was banished to Atlanta during the Federal occupancy of Natchez. One chamber at Rosalie is known as the Grant bedroom, since it was U. S. Grant's quarters for a brief period while he was en route from Vicksburg to New Orleans. The house served as Union officers' headquarters for months. The ornate gilt mirrors above the twin fireplaces in the drawing room on the first floor were buried on Fort Rosalie Hill during the war and returned to the house afterward.

The Civil War was Rosalie's only brush with military affairs, which left the mansion unscathed to survive as an American's memorial, in name and location, to the conflicts that determined the destiny of the lower Mississippi Valley.

The Natchez Trace was the much-traveled, bandit-infested route into the heart of the lower Mississippi Valley for the Anglo-Americans who began to inundate this predominately French and Spanish world at the close of the eighteenth century. The forest road from Natchez to Nashville was primarily a return route for the flatboat men who floated their cargoes down to New Orleans. It also was the haunt of some of the roughest characters in early America. There was no law except a man's knife or gun.

Several dwellings that also served as taverns along the Trace survive in and near Natchez. The largest and most famous of these early buildings sits atop strategic Ellicott Hill within the city. Connelly's Tavern has none of the monumental grandeur found in the great antebellum mansions for which Natchez is famous. They were the product of wealth that came a generation or two later. But it offered elegance and safety that were outstanding in the river town's early days.

James Griffin designed and built Peter Little's Federal-period mansion, Rosalie, in Natchez in 1820. The name was derived from the site, location of the old French Fort Rosalie, where the destiny of the lower Mississippi Valley was decided.

Peter Little.

Eliza Little.

The Tavern is Natchez' best surviving example of the French influence on architecture, even though it was built for an American at a time when His Excellency Don Gayoso ruled the city for Spain. The hipped roof sweeping down over front and rear galleries and the timber construction above a lower story of brick are typical of the homes the French brought to the Valley. It obviously was designed by Creole carpenters, who probably used timbers from river flatboats in its construction.

The grant for the hilltop property, which required construction of a dwelling within a year, was made to a Mrs. Watts before 1795. Patrick Connelly acquired the handsomely built house before 1797. In that year Major Andrew Ellicott came to the inn and the hill

Connelly's Tavern, Natchez' best surviving example of the French influence on architecture, was built in 1795 and acquired by Patrick Connelly two years later. In the territory where the law was often a man's gun it became a refuge and a famous stopping-place for the gentlemen traveling downriver to the heart of the lower Mississippi Valley, or returning by land.

196

that bears his name. He was surveying for President Washington to determine the southern boundary of the United States and briefly flew the Stars and Stripes on the hill beside the Tavern in defiance of the Spanish flag still floating over Fort Rosalie. The official raising of the flag occurred a year later when Captain Isaac Guion and his troops took positions on the hill Ellicott had made famous and threatened to fire on Fort Rosalie unless the Spanish garrison evacuated territory rightfully a part of the United States.

Connelly's Tavern, which has a strange brick-lined moat protecting access from the hillside to the rear gallery and upper floor, welcomed many notable visitors to Natchez during its early years. Important persons such as France's Duc d'Orléans were entertained in the elegantly furnished quarters upstairs. Aaron Burr and his accomplice, Harman Blennerhasset, following the exposure of their plot against the government, are said to have schemed their defense in the basement tavern. This room today is ornamented with a bar brought

Aaron Burr.

from one of the rough-and-tumble saloons in Natchez-under-the-Hill, a notorious riverfront hell which in time was undercut and swallowed by the Mississippi.

Connelly's passed through many hands, being operated mostly as an inn, but also serving as a private home. It became a school and had reached tenement status by the time it was acquired and restored by the Natchez Garden Club. The building is open the year round.

Eighteen miles north of Natchez, where the deep ruts of the old Trace bend around a small knoll, the National Park Service has restored Mount Locust, which was a typical "stand," or "house of refreshment," on the long road that led to Nashville. Mount Locust was built sometime between 1777 and 1783 as a farm home, but soon became an inn, like almost every dwelling in the wilderness along the Trace.

197

The builder was either John Bloomart, a former warrant officer in the British navy, or his associate William Ferguson, a Tory who fled from Williamsburg, Virginia, during the Revolution. Bloomart first obtained the land from the Spaniards, but Ferguson apparently was the original occupant, taking title to the place in 1781 after Bloomart was convicted of conspiring against Spain and imprisoned at Havana.

Mount Locust was first known as Mound Plantation, since it is only a short distance from a high grass-covered pyramid erected on a hilltop by the ancestors of the sun-worshiping Natchez Indians. The design of Mount Locust follows the French pattern, with galleries or porches under a hipped roof. The structure is almost entirely built of sassafras timber — a circumstance that has aided in its preservation, since this pungent wood is remarkably resistant to decay.

Ferguson died in 1801, and his widow married James Chamberlain. The Chamberlains, when the Trace was most traveled in 1820 (just about the time the steamboats ended its usefulness as a return route upriver) added two rooms to the original three. The National Park Service has restored Mount Locust to its appearance at this period.

A Chamberlain descendant who is today a Park Service ranger lived in the house when it was acquired as part of the Natchez Trace historic highway. Mount Locust is furnished in keeping with its frontier character. It is open throughout the year.

Andrew Jackson — detail of an engraving
by J. B. Longacre after a drawing from life.

The Hermitage

The town of Nashville was just four years old when her most distinguished citizen, Andrew Jackson, became a resident in 1788. He crossed the mountains from North Carolina to the western reaches of the Cumberland River when he was twenty-one, armed with a political commission. The country was rough and tough, and so was the fiery young man who was to become the seventh President of the United States.

The story of The Hermitage began with Jackson's lodging at the widow Donelson's, a few miles east of Nashville. He fell in love with her daughter Rachel, who was estranged from her husband, a Kentuckian. Jackson and Rachel were married in 1791, believing that she had been granted a divorce. The decree, they later learned, had not become final, and a second ceremony was performed to legalize their marriage — a fact that Jackson's political enemies used against him all his life.

Jackson established a farm and store on land near his in-laws, the Donelsons, and in 1804 bought the site of The Hermitage in the same vicinity. He and Rachel moved into their first home on the farm, a two-story log house, in 1805. He set up a new store at nearby Clover Bottom. Here also was the community track where the grudge race won by his famous horse, Truxton, led to a duel in which Jackson, though wounded, killed Charles Dickinson.

The brick walls that form the central, two-story portion of The Hermitage were begun in 1819. Jackson was famed by then as Old Hickory, the general who had defeated the British at the battle of New Orleans. The Jacksons occupied this simple, rectangular home in

199

The widowed Jackson's hostess was his niece, Mrs. Emily Donelson, the wife of Andrew Jackson Donelson.

The seventh President of the United States began the building of The Hermitage in Nashville in 1819. Andrew and Rachel Jackson occupied a portion of it in 1821. After Rachel's death and a fire, the house was rebuilt in 1836 as a typical columned, ante-bellum plantation mansion of the South. The furnishings were brought from Philadelphia.

1821. Rachel, however, never saw The Hermitage in its final form. The flanking one-story wings and a classic portico were added in 1831, while Jackson was living at the White House. Rachel had died two years before, on the eve of his inauguration. He was still in Washington, in his second term as President, when fire swept The Hermitage in 1834. Jackson immediately instructed his adopted son, Andrew, Junior, to have the house rebuilt.

The Hermitage acquired its gleaming white façade and full two-story portico — typical of the South's ante-bellum plantation homes — in this reconstruction, which was not complete until 1836. The white paint, like that on the White House in Washington, was applied to cover the scorched but still serviceable masonry walls of the front façade. The interior was almost completely renewed. The younger Andrew's wife, on a visit to her family in Philadelphia, ordered furniture and fittings, which were shipped to New Orleans, and thence up the Mississippi, the Ohio, and the Cumberland to Nashville.

Fire again struck at Jackson. The steamboat and its cargo were destroyed at the dock in Nashville. Nearly every item had to be ordered from Philadelphia a second time. The striking pictorial French paper on the walls in the center hall, described as "3 sets of fine paper hanging, Views of Telemachus, @ $40, $120," was one of the items replaced. The first set had not burned, but was sold to a neighbor as salvage, much to the indignation of the Jacksons.

The Hermitage is furnished just as it was at the time of President Jackson's death in 1845. The state of Tennessee purchased the property in 1856, but providentially permitted the family to remain in the house during the long Reconstruction years that followed the Civil War. Both the state and the Jacksons were without funds. The younger Andrew's widow auctioned off the dining room furniture, which years later found its way back to the house from the neighboring families who had bought it.

Mrs. Andrew Jackson III was among those who rescued The Hermitage from neglect in 1889. She and other patriotic women formed the Ladies Hermitage Association, modeled on the organization that by then had insured the future of Mount Vernon. The Association keeps Old Hickory's home open throughout the year.

The
Bolduc House

The most interesting and truly French Colonial home is not in the bayou country of Louisiana but one of a group of old Creole dwellings in a little Missouri town not far south of Saint Louis. Sainte Genevieve was founded in 1735 by *habitants* who had come to the Illinois country from Canada. Their farm-village way of life and distinctive architecture live today in the Bolduc house.

Sainte Genevieve on the west bank of the Mississippi was an outgrowth of Kaskaskia on the east bank in Illinois. It was first known as Saint Joachim. The river that eventually engulfed old Kaskaskia nearly destroyed Sainte Genevieve in 1785. The following year the *habitants* began to move their houses to higher ground, where the town is located today. The oldest part of the Bolduc house, believed to have been built about 1770, was moved and rebuilt in this period.

Louis Bolduc, the owner, was a prosperous planter, lead miner, and merchant. He was born in Saint Joachim parish, Quebec, in 1734 and died at Sainte Genevieve in 1815. His large home — it measures eighty-two by forty-eight feet — is built of heavy vertical timbers on a stone foundation, a method of construction the French colonists called *poteaux sur solle*. The upright timbers are set only a few inches apart and chinked between with a mixture of clay and chopped straw known as *bouzillage*.

The ceiling of the oldest half of the house (Bolduc is thought to have doubled the size of his dwelling at the time of relocation) is also built of huge, adz-squared timbers. Above it are heavy oak trusses arranged in medieval Norman pattern to support the roof. Norman and French-Canadian custom called for a steep hipped roof, so that the thatch used in the Old World would shed water. The form persisted in America, where shingles soon replaced thatch. The addition of porches or galleries in the hot and rain-lashed Mississippi Valley brought further change. The steep roof was flattened out at the bottom like the rim of a hat to sweep out over the galleries.

Louis Bolduc's house was originally built about 1770 and moved in 1786 to its present site in Sainte Genevieve, Missouri. The house, garden, and picket fence illustrate early Creole life, as do the bedroom (*above*) and dining room (*below*).

The roof of the Bolduc house had been altered and covered with tin when the Missouri Colonial Dames obtained the property. It has been returned to its original, distinctively Creole appearance, including the *epis*, or finials, perched at either end of the ridge. These quaint and sometimes elaborately carved ornaments once were a familiar sight in France and parts of French Canada.

Bolduc's heirs built a stone kitchen and bake oven into a corner of their home in 1820, probably to replace a less convenient separate kitchen building. This addition, which interrupts the customary complete encirclement of the house by the gallery, is the only alteration of the original dwelling that has been retained in its restoration.

Sainte Genevieve preserved its French Colonial identity well into the American period after the Louisiana Purchase. Historian Henry M. Brackenridge, who had known the town in his youth, returned in 1811 and wrote that "the inclosures of pickets, the intermingled orchards and gardens, still gave a character distinct from American villages."

The high cedar picket fence, really a stockade, has been restored around the Bolduc house. A portion of the garden and orchard flourish again. French Colonial furniture, obtained from Canada, completes the early Creole scene indoors, where a few Bolduc family heirlooms are also preserved.

The Bolduc house, which is managed by the Woman's Club of Sainte Genevieve, is open from April 1 to November 1.

Robert Campbell — painting by
George Eichbaum, about 1859–1860.

Up the Big River

The Campbell House & Prairie du Chien

The great stainless steel arch on the banks of the Mississippi at Saint Louis is the National Park Service's memorial to Thomas Jefferson's vision and success in opening up the West. Saint Louis, as the arch suggests, was the gateway — the headquarters for the fur traders who blazed the trails across the Rockies and established the outposts that led to the Pacific Coast. The story of this conquest is portrayed in the Old Courthouse headquarters of the Jefferson National Expansion Memorial.

One of the legendary figures, a companion of Jim Bridger, Kit Carson, and other mountain men, was Robert Campbell. He came to Saint Louis from Ireland in 1824, was one of the organizers of the Rocky Mountain Fur Company and the daring commander of many trapper expeditions. Famous Fort Laramie, the Wyoming stronghold for countless emigrant wagon trains in later years, was established as one of his trading posts.

Campbell had made a fortune from beaver pelts by the time he was thirty-two, in 1836. He went into business in Saint Louis at that time, becoming the president of two banks and the owner of much real estate. When he was thirty-seven he married nineteen-year-old Virginia Jane Kyle, of North Carolina.

The Campbells bought their house on Lucas Place — now 1508 Locust Street — in 1854. It had been built only three years earlier and is typical of the early Victorian evolution from Greek Revival days. The exclusive residential enclave in which it was built has been swallowed up by the city today, and Campbell's home and garden, surrounded by an ornamental cast-iron fence, are the only survivals in that neighborhood of Saint Louis as it was one hundred years ago.

Adventurous Robert Campbell made his fortune as a fur trader in the West. He became one of the richest men in Saint Louis and bought his early Victorian house in 1854. After he and his wife had died, two recluse sons lived fifty years in the shuttered house, clinging to the past and their parents' possessions. Today the house stands as it was when Robert Campbell lived in it nearly a hundred years ago.

The home and its contents are exactly as Campbell knew them up to the time of his death in 1879. Mrs. Campbell died shortly after her husband, and two bachelor sons who survived her lived as wealthy recluses in the shuttered house for the next fifty years. Nothing was disturbed — the sons even saved all of their mother's dresses, including the faille and satin gown in which she had welcomed President and Mrs. Grant to the home as dinner guests.

The museum contents of the Campbell house were not revealed until the death of the last son in 1941. The estate put them up for auction. A group of local historians who called themselves the William Clark Society rounded up the money to buy five van loads of the Campbell antiques. They later organized a foundation to purchase the house, to which the Belter chairs, the carved piano, the gas chandeliers, and other appurtenances of early Victorian life have been returned.

The most unusual room in the house is the double parlor, which has two fireplaces along one wall, one on each side of a bay window opening on the garden. The French gold-leaf mirrors above the mantels, ornate brass and bronze chandeliers, and fine rosewood furniture also contribute to its mid-nineteenth-century elegance. The bog oak furniture in the dining room is thought to have been purchased in Ireland by Robert Campbell during one of the trips he made to his native land.

The garden at one side of the house was created by Campbell shortly after he moved to Lucas Place, when he bought the lot that adjoined his home. The extra lot also provided space for his carriage house, which had servants' rooms on its second floor. Mrs. Campbell's carriage, built in Saint Louis before the Civil War, was acquired with the house.

The Campbell House Foundation opens the house to the public every day of the week.

Villa Louis at Prairie du Chien, Wisconsin, is one of America's outstanding landmarks

208

of the Victorian age. But the ornate elegance it acquired after the Civil War was only the closing chapter in a long and romantic story.

French *voyageurs* named Prairie du Chien for Big Dog, a Fox Indian chief. The fertile grassy plain in the middle of the river, far below the high bluffs on either side, became a headquarters for the fur trade. It is only a short distance above the mouth of the Wisconsin River, where Joliet and Marquette first saw the Mississippi in 1673. They had traveled up the Fox River from Lake Michigan and portaged into the Wisconsin, opening a route through which millions of beaver and other pelts were ferried to the East in the next one hundred and fifty years.

The river-bottom prairie was a meeting place for the Indian tribes, spring and fall, long before the French came. Mound-builders lived there in ancient times. Villa Louis sits on the low crest of a mound. Two American forts occupied the site before the house: Fort Shelby, built in 1814 and burned the same year by the British; and Fort Crawford, which was rebuilt in another location after 1831.

The removal of Fort Crawford led to the purchase of the mound by Hercules Louis

The double parlor contains two fireplaces and is the most impressive room in the house. The French mirrors, elaborate chandeliers, and rosewood sofas and chairs preserve the ornately harmonious and elegant atmosphere of Saint Louis's golden Victorian years.

The charming statue in the drawing room of Villa Louis is of Virginia and Violet, granddaughters of the builder, who many years later led in restoring the house.

Villa Louis at Prairie du Chien was originally built by Hercules Louis Dousman, agent for John Jacob Astor, in 1843. The original red brick, two-story house, set on an Indian mound, was almost Georgian in its simplicity. Dousman married his partner's widow, who called the house Le Château Brillant and lit its glassed-in veranda with five hundred candles each night.

The son of the builder, Hercules Louis Dousman II, and his wife Nina, who named the house Villa Louis in honor of her husband and his father. The photographs were probably taken at Villa Louis in the early 1870s.

211

Dousman, who was agent for John Jacob Astor and the American Fur Company at Prairie du Chien. Dousman built the original Villa Louis in 1843. It was a big red-brick, two-story house, almost Georgian in its simplicity. A year later he brought his bride, the widow of his partner Joseph Rolette, to Le Château Brillant, as she called her new home. The house in its early form had a glassed-in porch along the front which required five hundred candles for illumination at night.

Madame Dousman remodeled the house to its present form in 1872, a few years after her husband's death. She completely renewed the interior with the massive and ornate woodwork of the Victorian period, added a third-floor ballroom, and sheathed the structure in properly "fashionable" yellow brick brought from Milwaukee. All the dependencies — her husband's office, where he dealt with Indians and *voyageurs*; an ice house that was used to air-condition the house; a laundry and wine cellar — were left as built originally.

Hercules Louis Dousman II, who inherited the property after his mother's death, was an ardent horseman and breeder of trotting horses. He built a cork-surfaced race track and huge stables before his death three years after taking possession. Only a carriage house remains as a reminder of his brief and fabulously spendthrift years.

His widow named "the house on the mound" Villa Louis to honor her husband and his father. Her son Louis De Verville Dousman was the last of the family to occupy the mansion, which came into the possession of the Wisconsin State Historical Society in 1952.

The furnishings in Villa Louis are mostly family heirlooms shown in a setting that faithfully mirrors the mid-Victorian age. Hercules Dousman's granddaughters, Mrs. F. R. Bigelow, and Mrs. Violet Dousman Young supervised and aided the restoration after the Dousman heirs established the house as a museum.

The Historical Society also maintains at Prairie du Chien one of the few remaining stone houses built by French *voyageurs* in the upper Mississippi valley. Michael Brisbois, from Maska, Quebec, settled on the island prairie in 1781. He was a fur trader and baker and built his plain little home of native stone at the water's edge between 1808 and 1815. As the English along the Atlantic Coast, when they were unable to find lime rock, had used oyster shells for lime mortar to bind bricks and stone, so Brisbois dredged and burned freshwater mussels from the river to make cement for the walls of his house. The pieces of shell are visible in mortar between stones.

Villa Louis and the Brisbois house are open every day from May 1 until November.

Ohio River Homes

J. F. D. Lanier's Mansion
&
The Taft Museum

Lanier is a family name to conjure with in the South, linked with the Washingtons and im-mortalized by Sidney Lanier, the poet and musician from Georgia. It is no surprise, there-fore, to discover that one of the handsomest ante-bellum Greek Revival homes along the southern reaches of the Ohio River was built by a Lanier. It is a surprise, however, to find the house on the north bank of the river in Indiana, and to learn that the builder, James F. D. Lanier, risked his considerable fortune to back the Union cause during the Civil War. Lanier's unsecured loans — more than a million dollars — enabled the almost bankrupt state of Indiana to equip troops and meet its obligations in the 1860s.

Lanier came to the little river town of Madison, Indiana, from North Carolina, where he was born in 1800, and went to Transylvania College, in Lexington, Kentucky, to ob-tain a law degree. When his parents brought him west in 1817 Madison was still a staging point for the settlers flooding the Northwest Territory. Indiana had just become a state, and Madison was both the destination for flatboats loaded with homesteaders coming down the Ohio and the port from which their produce was shipped down the Mississippi to the Gulf.

Steamboats powerful enough to travel upstream as well as down soon appeared. The booming commerce on the river and later investment in railroads was the basis of Lanier's success as a banker and financier. In 1840 he commissioned Francis Costigan, a builder-architect who had come from Baltimore to Madison, to design and erect his home. Taking full advantage of Madison's position on a narrow flat along the broad Ohio below four-hundred-foot-high cliffs, Lanier bought a city block at the water's edge. Costigan located the banker's mansion, with its stately portico, overlooking a long sweep of lawn, the river, and the distant cliffs that line the Kentucky shore.

Greek Revival architects usually sought to emulate ancient temples in their adaptions of classic design. Costigan, in the Lanier house, supported a massive entablature with the

James Lanier, who financed Indiana's part in the Civil War, commissioned Francis Costigan to design and build his beautiful Greek Revival mansion in Madison, Indiana, in 1840.

The graceful spiral staircase is set in a well in the center of the house and reaches up to an eight-sided glass cupola projecting above the building.

four thirty-foot-high Corinthian columns of the portico. He carried the entablature completely around the nearly square building and used the space it enclosed for third-floor rooms, which get their light through circular "porthole" windows.

The architect marked the completion of his job with a silver plate bearing his name and the date, 1844, on the newel post at the base of the graceful spiral stairs in the middle of the house. This staircase is set in a well that is topped by an eight-sided, glassed-in cupola projecting above the roof.

A Madison newspaper in 1844 noted that Costigan not only designed the Lanier residence but also executed much of the intricate carpentry with his own hands. In common with most builders of the period he probably relied on Asher Benjamin's design books but qualified as an architect in his originality as well. "Architecture," he philosophized, "like statuary, is a mute language that conveys unalterable impulses of thought to other minds, present and to come."

Financier Lanier moved his business to New York City in 1851 and left one of his sons, Alexander, to occupy the mansion in Madison. Four generations of the family lived in the house, which the state of Indiana acquired as a memorial in 1925. The furnishings in the high-ceilinged, elaborately corniced rooms are almost entirely family possessions. Some are from the Victorian era of the Alexander Laniers, but others belonged to his parents and were returned from James F. D. Lanier's dwelling in New York.

The portico that overlooks the river is ornamented by a fine wrought-iron railing reminiscent of those in New Orleans. The similarity is genuine, for many of the gates and balconies of New Orleans were fabricated in Madison and shipped down the Mississippi. The handsome ironwork that remains in Madison contributes to the charm of this little port of yesteryear, which seems more a part of the South than of Hoosierland.

This town in which many early nineteenth-century homes survive is proud enough of its heritage to have organized a corporation to preserve and restore them. The Jeremiah Sullivan home, a brick house of Federal design built in 1818, is a showpiece maintained by Historic Madison, Inc. Another Greek Revival mansion built by Costigan, the 1848 home of Captain Charles Shrewsbury, is privately owned but open to the public.

The Lanier mansion is managed by the Division of State Parks, Indiana Department of Conservation, and is open throughout the year.

214

The Taft Museum, considered by some the finest Federal-period dwelling built, was constructed in 1820 for Martin Baum. Mrs. Charles P. Taft's father bought the house in 1871. In the 1920s the Tafts gave it to the Cincinnati Institute of Fine Arts as a museum. The romantic landscape murals on the walls of the fanlighted entrance hall were painted by Robert S. Duncanson in 1843.

Art museums in most big cities are awesomely monumental buildings, ranging from Grecian temples to Frank Lloyd Wright's corkscrew in concrete known as the Solomon R. Guggenheim Museum — but not in Cincinnati. The Taft Museum in the heart of the Ohio River metropolis is one of the nation's handsomest homes, a survival of the city's early prosperity as the gateway to the lower Midwest. It is furnished and maintained in its historic character while also serving as a museum for the Cincinnati Institute of Fine Arts.

In 1820 Martin Baum began the construction of the white-painted wood-frame mansion at the corner of Pike and Symmes Streets that many architects have considered the finest dwelling built in the Federal period. Though the designer is unknown its classical perfection suggests that Benjamin Henry Latrobe, the architectural genius of the Jeffersonian era, might have drawn up the plans when he was in the Ohio River country shortly before his death.

Baum lost his home to the Bank of the United States soon after its completion in 1826; it was bought by Nicholas Longworth four years later. The Longworths sold the house to the

father of Mrs. Charles P. Taft in 1871. The Tafts deeded their home, their paintings and other works of art, and a million dollars, contingent on the gifts of others, to help found the Cincinnati Institute of Fine Arts in the 1920s.

The interior of the Baum-Taft mansion was restored to the graceful elegance it had had during the early classical years, to serve as a museum. It had been well preserved. All of the finely turned woodwork is original, with the exception of the mantels and chair rail, which were replaced. The three large rooms and the entrance hall in the central portion of the house have ceilings ornamented with classical moldings and the eagles so popular in Federal years. These large rooms and the smaller chambers in the wings have been carefully decorated with period draperies and furniture to contribute to the impression that the paintings on the walls and other objects of art are being viewed in the privacy of an early American home. White-painted woodwork and delicately tinted walls — carrying out the original color scheme — furnish a bright and pleasant background.

The paintings on the walls of the handsome fanlighted entrance hall are part of the

217

fabric of the house. These romantic landscapes and over-door decorations in rococo frames are murals, discovered under layers of paint and paper. They were commissioned by Nicholas Longworth from Robert S. Duncanson in 1843. Duncanson, the son of a Scottish father and Negro mother, was a popular artist in Cincinnati for a number of years and later worked in England.

The floor plan of the house is essentially unchanged from Baum's day. Mrs. Taft's father, David Sinton, built a rear addition to the north wing of the mansion, which is used for museum offices today. The dining room, at the rear of the south wing, was slightly enlarged by Mrs. Taft.

The Museum is open to the public, without charge, throughout the year; Sundays and holidays it is open only in the afternoons.

Adena

Adena, Thomas Worthington noted in his diary, was the ancient Hebrew word "given to places remarkable for the delightfulness of their situations." He and Mrs. Worthington therefore gave the name to their home near Chillicothe, Ohio, which they had first called Mount Prospect Hall.

Adena is indeed delightfully situated on a hill northwest of Chillicothe, overlooking the Scioto River valley and the town that was capital of the vast Northwest Territory and the first seat of government when Ohio became a state in 1803. The big stone house was built shortly afterward, reaching completion in 1807 while Worthington was serving as one of the two first senators from Ohio. He later served two terms as governor of the state and was five times elected to its legislature.

Worthington was born in Virginia's lower Shenandoah Valley, near Charles Town, which is now in West Virginia. He and his brother-in-law, Edward Tiffin, moved their families to Chillicothe in 1798, when the town was only two years old. The Scioto valley was the center of migration of the Jeffersonian Republicans from Virginia. Worthington and Tiffin took the lead in bringing Ohio into the Union. Tiffin was the first governor.

The Worthingtons moved to their hilltop estate in 1802, first living in a large log house. The construction of Adena began four years later, and their Federal-period home followed the Georgian traditions they had known in Virginia. Locally quarried freestone replaced the more conventional brick in the walls, and native walnut was cut for the woodwork — and painted, as was customary with pine in the East.

The plan of Adena and its outbuildings is that of a Virginia plantation. The two-story, hip-roofed house is flanked by lower wings which project at its front corners, providing an open court and porch at the entrance. Governor Worthington's study was located in one wing, while the kitchen and scullery occupied the other. The dependencies included a smokehouse and washhouse, with barns and servants' cabins considerably farther from the

The "door cupboard," a practical device for serving in the dining room, was designed by local carpenters, who also made the bedroom furniture.

The wallpaper and furnishings of the drawing room were shipped overland from Baltimore and Philadelphia. The portrait is of Thomas Worthington.

Adena, the delightfully situated home of Thomas Worthington, early senator from Ohio and twice its Governor, was built in 1807 on a hilltop near Chillicothe.

Thomas Worthington.

Eleanor Worthington.

house. The cabins would have been slave quarters in Virginia, but the Worthingtons had freed the Negroes that came with them to Ohio.

Mrs. Worthington employed German indentured servants to tend the gardens, which were planted with terraces to the east of the house, toward the Scioto valley. She imported many plants from the East and was particularly fond of roses. A collection of old-fashioned roses has been returned to the garden by the Ohio Historical Society, which restored and maintains Adena.

Much of the glass, wallpaper, marble for fireplaces, draperies, and furnishings was shipped overland to the Worthingtons — mostly from Baltimore and from Philadelphia. Local carpenters built some of the simpler bedroom furniture. A part of their handiwork is a handsome cherry "door cupboard" in the dining room. It has circular shelves that revolved into the entrance hall, where food was placed on them for serving.

This ingenious revolving cupboard is more reminiscent of the gadgetry of Thomas Jefferson than of the classic work of Benjamin H. Latrobe, exponent of the Greek Revival, who has been credited with the design of Adena. Worthington may have consulted Latrobe, but this feature of his home seems more like the work of the inventive owner.

Adena's builder died in 1827, but the home remained in the Worthington family until 1903, when it was purchased by Mr. and Mrs. George Hunter Smith of Chillicothe. Their daughter gave the property to the state of Ohio in 1946. The house is open from April through October, except Mondays.

VI

THE WEST

Seattle, Washington Territory, c. 1876.

Seattle, Washington Territory, c. 1876.

THE WEST

Permanent settlement of the northern plains and mountain valleys in the West came only yesterday, after the railroads were built. The early mountain men and wagon trains, except those of the Mormons, left little more than the sites of Army forts to mark their pioneering. Most of the homes that survive the initial settlement from Kansas to Washington State are from the years after the Civil War. They are architecturally akin to dwellings built farther east in the same mid-Victorian period, which is not within the scope of this book.

The Southwest, however, is marked by relics of a much earlier penetration of this vast, arid country where easy transport by water does not exist. They were left by the Spaniards, who had conquered Mexico by the middle of the sixteenth century and then sent their mission-building *padres* and military governors overland hundreds of miles to the north. Their adobe dwellings, in which the handiwork of the Indian builders and Spanish design were combined, first appeared in New Mexico, where missions were established in 1598. The Franciscans had Indian converts at work in almost all of New Mexico and in northern Arizona by the time the Pilgrims and the Puritans came to New England. The Palace of the Governors at Santa Fe (see page 237), built in 1610, is a survival of that first settlement.

The mark of Spain was left in Texas almost one hundred and fifty years later, centering in the missions established at San Antonio. Here too the link with Mexico was overland. Earlier outposts far up the rivers of East Texas, designed to counter the growing French influence in Louisiana, had only a brief life. The Indian influence is not apparent at San Antonio. The Governors' Palace there, built in 1749 (see page 233), is stone construction, as are the surviving, magnificently Spanish Baroque mission churches.

The *padres* built the California missions last of all, from 1769 into the early years of the nineteenth century. The threat of Russian occupation brought them north from Baja California. A group of reconstructed redwood buildings at Fort Ross, north of San Francisco, today marks the site of the Czar's lonely but significant little colony. It was abandoned in 1841 and the property sold to Johann August Sutter, the Swiss, whose independent colony eventually disrupted Mexican authority in California much more than the Russians had. His fort and home, together with relics of gold-rush days, can be seen in Sacramento.

The missions became the nucleus of California's towns and a source of land for the settlers who came in ever-growing numbers after Mexico supplanted Spain and began the secularization of Church property. The Hugo Reid adobe (see page 240), built on land that belonged to the mission San Gabriel, at Los Angeles, is typical of the humble Spanish-Indian dwellings of the early years. Governor Pico's home (1848) in Whittier and the Casa de Estudillo (1826) in San Diego are more pretentious Mexican homes, planned in the Spanish tradition to surround and open on a sheltered patio.

The Americans who came to California before its acquisition by the United States brought a new architectural influence. Nowhere is this more apparent than in Monterey, the Colonial and first territorial capital of California, which, like Charleston and Newport on the East Coast, lost its prominence almost overnight. San Francisco became the metropolis and Sacramento the capital of the gold-mad, golden state, and the old houses remained in Monterey because there was no economic incentive to replace them.

The economic incentive now exists, but Monterey has taken steps to preserve and capitalize on its architectural heritage. The Larkin house (see page 243) is considered the prototype of the Monterey style, which blends ideas from New England and Spanish Mexico. It is also a landmark in the history of America's great West. Its completion on the shores of the Pacific in 1838 by an American citizen and its subsequent use as the United States consulate in California were clear indications of how the West finally would be won.

Austin:

The French Legation

The pioneering Republic of Texas had a brief and stormy life from 1836 to 1845, when the Lone Star State joined the Union. The siege of the Alamo and the battle of San Jacinto marked its birth in blood. Conflict with marauding Indians and the displaced Mexicans was almost continuous, especially in Austin, the outpost capital on the banks of the Colorado River. But there were moments of almost comic relief.

The "pig incident" and "the archives war" both took place in Austin. The oldest home in the city, now a state museum administered by the Daughters of the Republic of Texas, was built in 1840 by the man involved with the pig. He was the Parisian Comte Alphonse Dubois de Saligny, and his Louisiana-Creole-styled mansion was the French Legation in the capital of the new nation in America's southwest.

The cultured de Saligny must have had great faith in Texas to return to Austin and build the house after the pig affair. It occurred in 1839 during his first visit to the capital, where the government conducted its business in a building surrounded by a stockade. His mission was to negotiate a loan from France to Texas. He lived briefly in an inn owned by Richard Bullock and then rented a nearby dwelling. But his former landlord kept pigs at the inn, and one of the animals got into a grain bin in de Saligny's stable. A servant of the count's killed the pig. Bullock then thrashed the servant and later ejected the protesting count from his inn, whereupon the outraged de Saligny broke off negotiations with President Mirabeau Lamar and his cabinet and retired to more civilized New Orleans — only to return the following year as chargé d'affaires and purchase land for the consulate.

The French Legation is built of fine-grained pine cut at Bastrop, a few miles down the Colorado River; the hardware was imported from France. The interior walls were not plastered but lined with heavy canvas, which was then painted; de Saligny utilized a heavy grade of cloth introduced into Texas by the Spaniards for use in controlling irrigation

Comte Alphonse Dubois de Saligny.

Parisian Comte Alphonse Dubois de Saligny was sent as chargé d'affaires to Austin, the capital of the new nation, Texas. He built the French Legation in 1840, modeling it on the Creole design then fashionable in Louisiana. The house was of fine-grained Bastrop pine; the walls were lined with heavy painted canvas, and the hardware was imported from France. With furnishings brought from New Orleans he tried to create an atmosphere in which to entertain and receive formally.

230

water. He planned his quarters with a large center hall, which he used for dining and for receptions and dancing. A formal parlor and a small rear study are on one side of the hall, two bedrooms on the other. The upper floor housed his servants, and the basement his wine cellar.

De Saligny's consulate never belonged to King Louis Philippe or his government, and only briefly to the count. He sold it to John Marri Odin, Roman Catholic vice-prefect apostolate who soon was ordained bishop of Texas, under an agreement providing for his own continued occupancy for at least two years. Bishop Odin in turn sold at a loss in 1847, when Austin was nearly deserted because of Indian raids and the war with Mexico. The consulate then became the home of the Robertson family, from whom the state of Texas obtained it in 1945.

"The archives war" pitted Texan against Texan during an earlier desertion in Austin's precarious early days. The Mexican army had seized San Antonio in 1842, and a detachment was rumored on its way to Austin. President Sam Houston removed his government to the city bearing his name. The Republic's archives were left in Austin, however, and President Houston sent a company of rangers to retrieve them.

The diehards remaining in Austin feared that if they lost the national archives Austin would be abandoned as the capital. A Mrs. Eberly is said to have fired a cannon at the rangers as their wagons hauled the records out of town. A posse from Austin later overtook them and returned the archives to the city.

The state government returned to Austin after the Mexican War. A handful of old homes built in the Greek Revival period before the Civil War survive in the city. The porticoed Governor's Mansion near the Capitol is the most notable, and was finished in 1856. The French Legation, however, is the sole survivor of the days when the leaders of the Republic met behind a stockade. It is open to the public throughout the year.

San Antonio:

The Governors' Palace

Military Plaza, San Antonio, Texas, 1852.

The presence of the Spanish dons and padres is felt in San Antonio perhaps more than in any big city within the United States. It was New Spain's most prosperous settlement east of the Rockies and north of the Rio Grande — first a stronghold against the French and then the center of Mexican resistance to the Anglo-American invasion that created Texas. San Antonio has preserved both spirit and buildings from this colorful past.

The mission churches and the Governors' Palace are the city's principal architectural heritage from the past. The Alamo, for instance, was a mission church known as San Antonio de los Alamos (cottonwoods) when the Franciscans completed it in 1757. Five years later its roof collapsed. The structure was a crumbling ruin in 1836 when Antonio López de Santa Anna wiped out the besieged Texans within its walls. The site is the spot where the original mission of San Antonio de Valero was established in 1718 by Father Olivares. That mission and the little town — Villa de Bexar — which Governor Alarcón staked out on the west side of the San Antonio River were the beginnings of the city.

Four additional missions strung out along the river south of San Antonio were built or building by 1731, and the church centers of all of them have been preserved. The entire mission compound has been restored and reconstructed at spectacular San José. The elaborate stone carving that frames the entrance to the church and a circular window above — the work of a sculptor the padres brought from Spain in the 1720s — rivals the finest that survives from Spain's colonial empire.

233

The spirit of Spain's early Colonial days in San Antonio is preserved in the Governor's Palace where civil and military affairs were conducted. The single-storied stone building is lime-plastered, with spouts that project from the walls for draining the roof; wrought-iron grilles cover the windows, and the date 1749 is inscribed above the beautifully carved wooden door.

One of the bedrooms (*left*) has an open charcoal brazier for heating. From the entrance the stairway to the loft can be seen (*above right*). In the Room of the Blessed Virgin (*right*) a shrine was maintained for worship.

The single-storied Governors' Palace faces the Military Plaza in that part of San Antonio which was first called Bejar, or Bexar. Here a long succession of vice-governors and governors lived and conducted civil and military affairs. They also perpetuated a quarrel over the shared authority between Church and state that began with Governor Alarcón and Father Olivares and did not end until the close of the eighteenth century, when the missions abandoned attempts to regulate as well as convert the Indians.

The keystone above the Palace's massive entrance door bears the date 1749 and the Hapsburg coat of arms. The walls are stone, lime-plastered, and rise in a parapet above the flat roof, which is drained by the projecting *canales,* or downspouts, Spanish builders typically employed. The windows are protected by wrought-iron grilles.

There are ten rooms floored with tile and flagstone, with cypress rafters overhead. Both the *comedor* (dining room) and *sala de baile* (ballroom) have hooded fireplaces. The *sala de recepción* in the rear of the ballroom opens to a patio, with the walled garden beyond.

The old Palace became the property of the Perez family early in the nineteenth century and was converted at various times in the next century into a second-hand clothing store, a bar, and a café. It was bought by the city of San Antonio in 1929 and restored to the status it enjoyed when San Antonio de Bexar was the capital of New Spain's Province of Texas. The building is open throughout the year.

General Stephen Watts Kearny and his troops occupied the Palace for the United States in 1846.

Santa Fe:

Palace of the Governors

Santa Fe may not be as ancient a community as Saint Augustine, but its Palace of the Governors of New Mexico is certainly the oldest dwelling built by white men on continental United States soil. The long, low adobe building was the principal structure of the *Casas Reales,* or Royal Houses, which Don Pedro de Peralta erected to fortify the town he established in 1610.

The design belonged to Don Pedro and his Spanish officers, but the construction relied on methods the Pueblo Indians had employed for centuries. Indian laborers shaped the baked mud walls and roofed the Palace with heavy clay on a thatch of poles supported by huge *vigas,* or beams, which projected at ceiling height on both sides of the building. They are now cut off and protected with plaster. The principal improvements the Spaniards introduced were casting the adobe in bricks beforehand instead of puddling the walls, and the use of wood corbels, or brackets, to give the *vigas* better support.

The Palace is the prototype of the most truly American of architectural forms — the combination of Indian and Spanish design that belongs to the Southwest. It is also a survival of the most northerly and successful settlement of Spain in North America, excepting the much later migration up the California coast. Don Pedro's Santa Fe was the capital of a seventeenth-century province that knew no northern boundary and reached from the Mississippi to the Pacific.

237

Governor Don Diego de Vargas Azpata Lufan Ponce de Leon recaptured the Palace from the Indians, after twelve years of occupation.

The gold the Spaniards had sought from the days of Coronado was hard to find, but the soul-saving padres enjoyed apparent success. A score of missions were established in the first twenty years, and tens of thousands of Indians were recorded as converts. In 1680, however, the Pueblos revolted and a thousand colonists were besieged in the Palace of the Governors. Hundreds who failed to reach the *Casas Reales* were killed. The Spaniards eventually broke out and retreated south to El Paso. The Palace and its walled patio became a fortified Indian *pueblo*, including a *kiva* — or heathen temple.

Spanish Governor Diego de Vargas, leader of the expedition that returned to New Mexico twelve years later, was unable to take the Palace stronghold by direct assault. His siege was not successful until he cut off the Indians' water supply — repeating a strategy the Pueblos had employed when they drove the Spaniards from Santa Fe.

The Palace and its associated buildings were described at that time as forming a quadrangle about a central patio, with towers at each of the corners. The walls connecting the

238

Santa Fe's Palace of the Governors is probably the oldest dwelling built by white men in the United States in a truly American architectural form. The old adobe-type structure was designed by Don Pedro de Peralta and his Spanish officers, who used Indian labor and methods of construction.

buildings and the towers were allowed to crumble after the Spanish troops returned, and a much larger military establishment was built. The Palace served only as the governor's office and residence thereafter.

Thirty Spanish governors occupied the old dwelling in Santa Fe in the succeeding one hundred and thirty years. Twenty-three had lived there before the Indian uprising. Fourteen Mexican governors were in residence during the period from 1822 to 1846, when trade with the Americans to the east began to displace Santa Fe's traditional reliance on Mexico.

The American occupation of the Palace began in 1846 with General Stephen Watts Kearny, who took over in a remarkably peaceful conquest. No shots were fired when his troops marched into Santa Fe. Kearny had supper with the Mexican Lieutenant-Governor and afterward raised the United States flag above the Palace. Twenty-four territorial and state governors thereafter occupied the Palace until its use for official business was abandoned in 1900. The Museum of New Mexico was established in the building in 1909.

Home of the
"Scottish *Paisano*"

Hugo Reid Adobe

Santa Anita, just east of Los Angeles and Pasadena, has been linked with thoroughbred racing for almost a century. Fast horses were a hobby with E. J. "Lucky" Baldwin, who, in 1870, bought the land where the present fabulously popular racetrack continues "to improve the breed."

Baldwin's huge Rancho Santa Anita, however, was not assembled by him, and race horses are only a part of its colorful history. Most of the original thirteen thousand acres are now covered by homes. One hundred and twenty-seven acres not far from the racetrack have been designated as the Los Angeles State and County Arboretum. Here, in the midest of the lavish plantings Baldwin made, the first adobe home and headquarters for Rancho Santa Anita has been restored.

Southern California's "Scottish *paisano*," Hugo Reid, was the builder. Reid came to Los Angeles in 1834. His home was Cardross, Scotland; he had studied at Cambridge and migrated north to California after living in South America and Mexico. His store and warehouse in the little *pueblo* of Los Angeles were successful, and in 1837 he was baptized at the mission and married a beautiful Indian princess, a widow with four children who was a devout Roman Catholic. Don Perfecto Reid, as he now called himself, was a leader in the community and acquired by grant from the Mexican government nearly half the present city of Pasadena. Rancho Santa Anita had been mission land. The little *casa* at the edge of the spring-fed pond on the ranch grew to its present size between 1839 and 1841, as the Reids spent more and more of their time at this isolated oasis rather than in the house they owned in town.

The flat roof of the little three-room house is built of tule stalks laid across the rafters and covered with tar from the La Brea pits, a natural resource that was much used in early Los Angeles. The walled patio is sheltered by thatched tule. The thick adobe brick walls have the usual coating of lime mortar to protect them from the rain.

240

Hugo Reid, a Scot who became known as "Don Perfecto," built his adobe house in 1839 on the Rancho Santa Anita granted him by the Mexican government. In 1870 E. J. "Lucky" Baldwin, whose hobby was breeding fast horses, bought the land. Today it is the site of famous Santa Anita racetrack. Reid's three-room, thick-walled adobe house in an arboretum nearby recalls the days when his cattle grazed on the present site of Pasadena.

The flat roof is made of tule stalks covered with tar.

The furniture in Reid's restored adobe, a gift of the Los Angeles Colonial Dames, is the sort of mixture that might have been accumulated by the Scottish *paisano* and his Doña Victoria, as she became known to honor her husband's favorite queen. The rather plain, farmhouse-type pieces are from Spanish, English, and New England sources. Indian blankets, rugs, and pottery are included.

Reid spent the last two years of his short and remarkable life writing an account of the Gabrieleno Indians — the tribe to which his wife belonged. He had lost most of his fortune in a series of disastrous trading ventures, including voyages to Hawaii and China. He sold Rancho Santa Anita for twenty cents an acre in 1847. Reid was a delegate to the state constitutional convention in Monterey in 1850 and died at the age of forty-two in 1852. Doña Victoria, the Princess Bartolomea, survived him by sixteen years.

Rancho Santa Anita, after Hugo Reid, continued to set the pace in the development of Southern California. The Scottish *paisano* had populated the rolling valley acres in the lee of the San Gabriel mountains with herds of cattle. In 1857 one of the subsequent owners of the ranch, William Wolfskill, set out acres of orange trees. His was the first extensive planting of citrus fruit in the valley and the beginning of a huge industry that has now almost vanished from the high-priced land near Los Angeles.

Lucky Baldwin did not disturb the crumbling old adobe near the pond, but it was nearly in ruins when the Arboretum was established. The basic structure was preserved, however, and finally restored to the simple type of dwelling the Scottish *paisano* and his friends, the mission Indians, had learned to build from the Spaniards who settled in California. The Arboretum and the Hugo Reid adobe are open every day all year.

The
Larkin House,
Monterey

The Larkin house at Monterey is famous on two counts — as the home of a shrewd, straightforward Yankee who was the central figure in California's acquisition by the United States and as the prototype of countless "Monterey type" homes in which the architecture of Spain and New England are handsomely blended.

Thomas O. Larkin came to Monterey from Boston in 1832. About two years later he began construction of his home, which also housed his trading post stocked with goods brought by clipper ships around the Horn. His meticulous account books indicate that the structure, including land and outbuildings, was completed in 1837 at a cost of five thousand dollars.

Larkin became a respected and fabulously successful business leader in somnolent little Monterey, which Spain and Mexico had maintained as California's port of entry and capital since its founding in 1770. He did not become a Mexican citizen and even contrived to marry under the American flag. The ceremony was performed offshore by the captain of the vessel that brought his bride, the young widow of a New England sea-captain, from Hawaii.

During the crucial years 1843 to 1846 President John Tyler appointed Larkin the first and only United States consul in Monterey. Eugène Duflot de Mofras, a French attaché living in Monterey, had earlier informed his government, "It is the lot of this province to be conquered." Larkin's services to the United States began long before his appointment as consul, however. The Yankee trader's home was almost a command post for the procession of navy and army commanders who maintained a sort of death watch on the fading Mexican government in California.

In 1842 Commodore Thomas Ap Catesby Jones landed marines and seized Monterey without a shot, mistakenly assuming that war with Mexico had begun and that the British fleet in the Pacific had orders to invade. But the Stars and Stripes flew over the town on

Thomas O. Larkin was the first and only United States consul to Mexico in Monterey. He was a shrewd and wealthy Yankee traveler and a central figure in California's acquisition by the United States.

Spain's and New England's architectural styles are beautifully combined in the Larkin adobe house, built in 1835. It was the first of the popular "Monterey type," which blends a front-entrance, center-hall plan with first- and second-floor galleries and a walled-in patio at the side and in the rear. The living room (*left*) is furnished with eighteenth-century family heirlooms.

that first occasion for only a day. Larkin was the intermediary who persuaded Jones that an apology and retirement were in order at that stage of the game. Not until 1846, when war was declared, was the consulate in Monterey openly proclaimed headquarters for American military governors.

John Charles Frémont was a frequent visitor and profited by the luck that usually attended his friend's business deals. He gave Larkin thirty-five hundred dollars to invest in a ranch, and Larkin bought land in the remote foothills of the Sierras, much to Frémont's distress. Within a few years, however, gold was discovered on the ranch, making General Frémont a millionaire.

Larkin's home is built of adobe bricks, with walls three feet thick. The floor plan is the familiar center-hall arrangement, brought from the East Coast, which Larkin and his Ladino carpenters surrounded with a first-floor veranda and second-floor balcony on three sides. The rear opens to a walled patio. He topped his dwelling with a flat-pitch hipped roof, which extends over the balcony.

Larkin's reputation as California's first millionaire was only begun in Monterey. His interests inevitably shifted to the Bay area after the gold rush began, and he eventually traded the house in Monterey for property in San Francisco. His granddaughter, Mrs. Harry S. Toulmin, brought the old home back into the family many years later. Mrs. Toulmin gave the restored and heirloom-furnished house to the State of California. It is open Wednesdays through Sundays all year.

GLOSSARY

THE EUROPEAN ORIGINS

Frequent reference has been made in this book to skills and customs the first settlers brought to America from their homelands. Some of the surviving early Colonial houses are almost replicas of farm and village cottages in Europe. These modest dwellings in England, France, and the Low Countries were all medieval in character. The architectural ideas of the Renaissance — derived from the classical orders of Greece and Rome — were either unknown to or beyond the reach of middle-class colonists, and therefore were long delayed in reaching America.

FROM ENGLAND

Tudor and earlier dwellings in the southeast counties of Britain were models for the English colonists who built along the Atlantic coast from Maine to the Carolinas in the seventeenth century. The wood house using a framework of heavy oak posts and beams, called girts, quite

similar to the steel frame in a modern skyscraper, dominated in New England. (See Fairbanks Homestead, page 20, and Buttolph-Williams House, page 65, for similarity to prototype.)

The medieval overhang of the second story persisted in America for almost a century. The plaster on the first-story wall of the English cottage covers clay and wattle, or soft brick "nogging." Similar fill was used in the earliest

American homes, but protected by wood siding, which was plentiful in the New World. Roofs steeply pitched for thatch or tile in England were soon shingled in the Colonies but retained their steep slopes for several generations. Post and girt construction persisted into the 1800s. The massive central chimney lost favor when Georgian center halls and stairways were introduced.

The cottage with chimneys at each gable end is the Old World prototype of the surviving seventeenth-century houses in Maryland and Virginia. (See Adam Thoroughgood House, page 159.) Frame houses apparently were built by the early generations of colonists in the

South, but did not endure the climate as well as in the North. Brick was more substantial. The end chimneys encouraged the development of the center hall with a back door (an American innovation) as well as a front opening so that cooling air would circulate in the summer.

FROM HOLLAND

The Dutch brought a love for ornamental brickwork and intricate "stepped" gables to the Hudson Valley. Very little of this delightful craftsmanship, which was concentrated in

the cities, has escaped demolition. Fort Crailo (see page 75) and a few farm houses with pleasantly patterned brick walls are left in the upper

Valley. The snug stone cottages built by early Dutch and Huguenot-Walloon families in country villages are those that have survived.

FROM FRANCE

France's contribution to early American architecture came to the Mississippi Valley both from Canada and from the West Indies. The cottage with a characteristic hipped roof is still in evidence from Missouri to Louisiana. The surrounding galleries, which added a "hat-brim" flare to the covering roof, apparently migrated to the Valley with colonists who had developed this hot-climate addition at French settlements in the Caribbean. The earliest homes, like their Norman prototypes, were built with upright post walls. The few traces

of this construction that survive (see Bolduc House, page 203) are covered with plaster or siding. When the cottage was raised on a high brick foundation, as in Louisiana, a ground floor was created and outdoor stairs to the upper living quarters were built into the gallery. The open gallery stairs persisted through many architectural periods in New Orleans.

CLUES TO
THE MAJOR PERIODS
IN EARLY AMERICAN
HOME DESIGN

The date of construction of American homes built before the Victorian period often cannot be determined by their appearance alone. Earlier styles and building practices often persisted as the wilderness was settled from east to west. But the pioneer years can be separated into four major architectural periods. Each covers an overlapping span of years.

The early Colonial began with the first generation of settlers and lingered into the early years of the eighteenth century. Georgian design supplanted this early, medieval-type construction and became almost universal during the later Colonial years. It remained popular immediately after the Revolution and then blended into Federal design (1800–1830). The fourth period was the Greek Revival (1830–1850).

Doorways, windows, and stairways are prominent architectural details. The illustrations show examples from each of the four periods. Similar design and construction will help to identify the period of a house — always provided that these parts of the structure are original, or restorations of the original, and not replacements installed during a later remodeling.

DOORWAYS

[1.] A plain batten door, made by layering two thicknesses of boards together, is the strictly utilitarian feature of early Colonial homes. The prominent studs in this example are the heads of the nails that fasten the outer layer of vertical boards to the inner planks. The frame is a simple enclosure. Ornamentation is absent, although the studs and wrought-iron pull display attractive craftsmanship.

[2.] The Georgian entranceway is meticulously, often elaborately, stylistic. This example from a house built in 1750 is topped by a broken serpentine pediment. The doorway is flanked by fluted pilasters. The gable pediment, shaped like a flattened letter A, is the most frequently

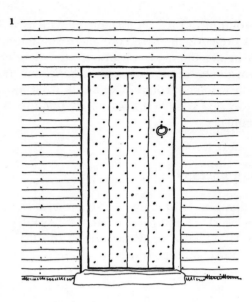

encountered headpiece above the doorway of less pretentious Georgian homes. The six panels in the door are planed from wood thick enough for the outer surface of the panel to be flush with the surface of the rest of the door.

[3.] Refinement and more imaginative use of classical forms came with the Federal period. The elliptical fanlight that serves as a headpiece is an especially graceful innovation, supported by the tracery of side lights set between severely plain pairs of pilasters. Fanlights no

wider than the width of the door and set immediately above it had a vogue in late Georgian years. But they were just a part of the bolder over-all design. Here the expansion of glass area is used to create the basic elements of the entranceway.

[4.] The Greek Revival embellished American homes with classical temple forms. The fashion

flourished with the new availability of mill-finished woodwork. Doors with raised panels were replaced by new designs in which the depressed panels are ornamented by applied strips

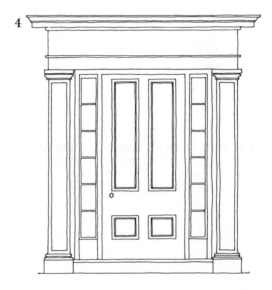

of molding. The other elements of this doorway — the headpiece cornice and frieze, and the open pilasters — are built up in similar fashion. The new design relied on new techniques.

WINDOWS

[1.] The most popular eighteenth-century improvement was the enlargement of windows and removal from early Colonial houses of the type of casement sash shown. None of the original casements survive in use, though many replicas have been installed. Casements often were fixed or had only one sash hinged. Sliding sashes also were used.

1

were thinned. The sashes shown are double-hung, and the introduction of weights to counterbalance top and bottom sashes required a box-type frame with space for the weights, instead of a solid member. The keystone lintel ornaments Georgian as well as Federal structures.

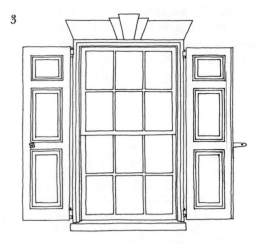

3

[2.] The Georgian period introduced twin sashes with much larger panes of glass, or lights, set in wood muntins. The sashes are enclosed in a frame planed from solid timbers, joined with wood pegs at the corners. They are single-hung — that is, only the bottom sash is movable. The flat segmental brick arch is typical of early Georgian buildings.

[4.] The trend to larger lights and thinned muntins continued during the Greek Revival. The lintels above the windows acquired prominence that carried over into Victorian times. The scroll-cut Greek key is typical. Louvered Venetian shutters became increasingly popular before 1850.

2

4

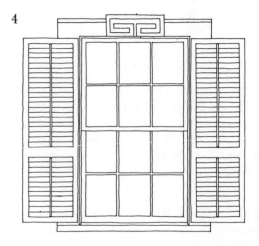

[3.] The glass lights were enlarged in Federal homes, while the wood muntins between them

[1.] Early Colonial New England homes usually have a winding staircase to the second floor in the narrow space between the front door and the wall of the massive center chimney. The stairs have a straight rise in the short stretch along the chimney wall, where the handrail rests on the handsomely turned stubby balusters. They then turn right again to reach the corridor across the front of the house.

[2.] The "winders" in eighteenth-century Georgian city tenements and small cottages fit into remarkably small space. The door at left opens on basement stairs which wind directly under the steps that circle steeply to the second floor. The two-panel doors, H-L hinges, and wrought-iron latches are typical.

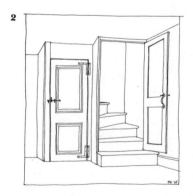

[3.] Formal stairways ornamented Colonial mansions, and Georgian design provided the setting in a center hall. Mahogany was favored for the broad handrail. Balusters often were elaborately turned. The exposed "open-string" step ends were ornamented with scroll-work or paneling.

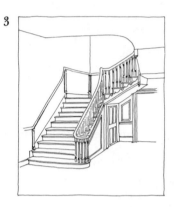

[4.] Stairways took light and graceful form in both Federal and Greek Revival homes. Curving lines predominate, often sweeping up in circles — occasionally in "flying" form, free from a supporting wall. Handrails and balusters were thinned.

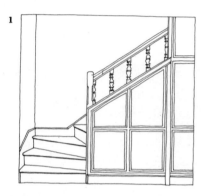

253

The early tides of conquest and settlement left their architectural marks in the United States. The boundaries indicate the areas penetrated by different nationalities from the beginning of the seventeenth century until just before the Revolution. Their influence is visible in buildings that survive in each area, although gradually modified by British design and practices that Anglo-Americans carried to the Pacific before the Mexican War. Some of the points of settlement, with founding dates, are listed below. Houses described in this book are found in most of these areas.

ENGLISH
Portsmouth, N.H. (1630)
Salem, Mass. (1628)
Boston, Mass. (1630)
Plymouth, Mass. (1620)
Providence, R.I. (1636)
Wethersfield, Conn. (1634)
Philadelphia, Pa. (1682)
Annapolis, Md. (1648)
Jamestown, Va. (1607)
New Bern, N.C. (1710)
Charleston, S.C. (1670)
Savannah, Ga. (1733)

DUTCH
Albany, N.Y. (1614)
New York City (1626)
New Castle, Del. (1638)

SWEDISH
Chester, Pa. (1643)

FRENCH
Niagara, N. Y. (1726)
Detroit, Mich. (1701)
St. Louis, Mo. (1764)
Ste. Genevieve, Mo. (1735)
Natchez, Miss. (1714)
New Orleans, La. (1718)
Mobile, Ala. (1701)

SPANISH
Saint Augustine, Fla. (1565)
San Antonio, Tex. (1718)
Santa Fe, N.M. (1610)
Tucson, Ariz. (1700)
Monterey, Calif. (1770)
San Gabriel (Los Angeles),
    Calif. (1771)

254

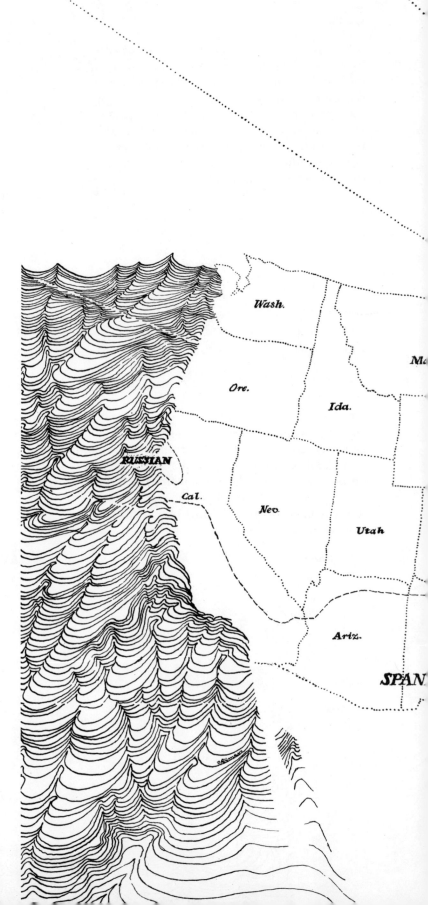

The Tides of Settlement

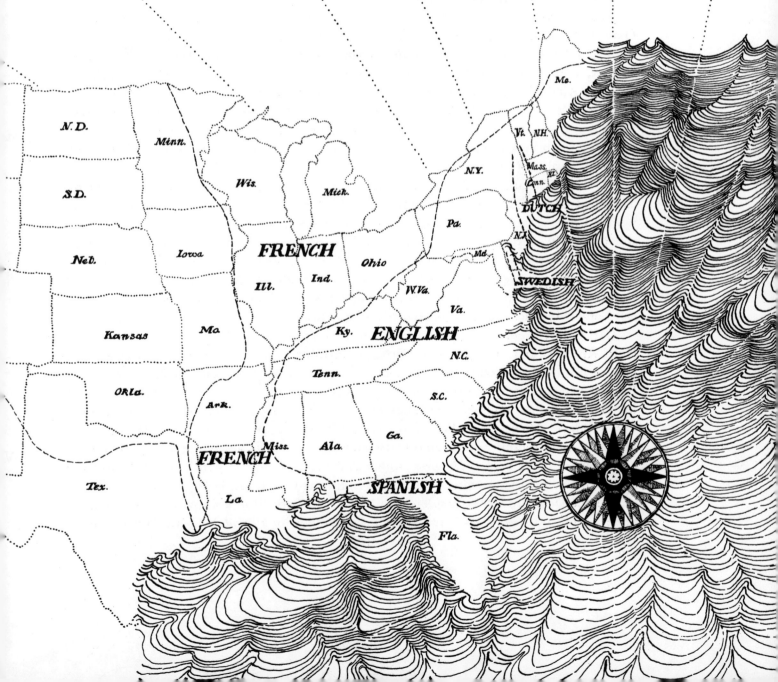

N.D.

Minn.

S.D.

Wis.

Mich.

Neb.

Iowa

FRENCH

Ind.

Ohio

Ill.

Kansas

Mo.

Ky.

ENGLISH

N.C.

W.Va.

Va.

Tenn.

S.C.

ORla.

Ark.

Ga.

FRENCH

Miss.

Ala.

Tex.

La.

SPANISH

Fla.

Me.

Vt. NH.

N.Y.

Mass.

Conn.

R.I.

DUTCH

Pa.

N.J.

Md.

SWEDISH

Bibliography

A complete bibliography of source material for this book would reach unwieldy proportions. It would be top-heavy with histories and biographies from which the contributions were minor, as well as with pamphlets and periodicals not readily available.

A reading list has been prepared instead. The titles and authors listed were major sources and offer a rich variety of text and illustration dealing with America's architectural history. The list begins with publications of general interest, followed by those concerned with regions or localities. Pamphlets and books about individual houses are not listed. They are usually available on the premises.

First on the list is Professor Hugh Morrison's *Early American Architecture* (New York: Oxford University Press, 1952), thorough and readable but regrettably not carried beyond the Federal period. *Architecture, Ambition and Americans* by Wayne Andrews (New York: Harper, 1955) carries on to recent years. *Domestic Architecture of the American Colonies* by Fiske Kimball (New York: Charles Scribner's Sons, 1922) and *The Dwellings of Colonial America* by Thomas T. Waterman (Chapel Hill: University of North Carolina Press, 1950) are valuable texts. *A Treasury of Early American Homes* by Dorothy and Richard Pratt (New York: Hawthorn Books, 1955) is a magnificent color picture book through Greek Revival times.

For New England Abbott Lowell Cummings has prepared a helping primer on *Architecture in Early New England* (a pamphlet published by Old Sturbridge Village in 1958). Samuel Chamberlain's outstanding photographic records of New England homes are available by locality, in many books. Notable within their states are Antoinette Forrester Downing's *Early Homes of Rhode Island* (Richmond, Va.: Garrett and Massie, 1937) and *The Architectural Heritage of Newport*, with Vincent J. Scully, Jr. (Cambridge, Mass.: Harvard University Press, 1952), and Connecticut Booklet No. 4 (Pequot Press, Stonington), the reprint of J. Frederick Kelly's *Connecticut's Old Houses*.

Carl Carmer's perceptive account of New York's past in *The Hudson River* (New York: Holt, Rinehart and Winston, 1962) prompts mention of the Rivers of America series as helpful historic background in other regions. Early New York and Philadelphia live in Carl Bridenbaugh's *Cities in the Wilderness* (New York: Alfred A. Knopf, 1955), and other books by the same author help re-create Colonial life and customs. *Dutch Houses in the Hudson Valley before 1776* by Helen Wilkinson Reynolds (New York: Payson and Clark, 1929) is a thorough architectural record. Harold Donaldson Eberlein produced three volumes on historic houses in New York — *Historic Houses of the Hudson Valley*, with Cortlandt Van Dyke Hubbard (New York: Architectural Book Publishing Co., 1942), being the most recent.

For the Delaware Valley Eberlein and Hubbard's *Portrait of a Colonial City* (Philadelphia: Lippincott, 1938) and *The Colonial Architecture of Philadelphia* by Frank Cousins and Phil M. Riley (Boston: Little, Brown, 1920) are standard references. More recent is *Historic Philadelphia* (Philadelphia: American Philosophical Society, 1953).

Tidewater homes and history are found in *The Mansions of Virginia* by T. T. Waterman (Chapel Hill: University of North Carolina Press, 1946); *Early Manor and Plantation Houses of Maryland* by Henry Chandlee Forman (1934); and *Homes of the Cavaliers* by Katherine Scarborough (New York: Macmillan, 1930). The architectural history of cities farther south is traced in *Architects of Charleston* by Beatrice St. Julien Ravenel (Charleston: Carolina Art Association, 1945) and *The Houses of Saint Augustine* by Albert Manucy (Saint Augustine Historical Society, 1962).

For west of the Appalachians Rexford Newcomb's *Architecture of the Old Northwest Territory* (University of Chicago Press, 1950) covers the region north of the Ohio to Minnesota. Nothing as comprehensive has been assembled for the lower Mississippi Valley. *Spanish Colonial Architecture in the United States* by Newcomb (New York: J. J. Augustin, 1937) and Trent Sanford's *Architecture of the Southwest* (New York: W. W. Norton, 1950) carry the story from Texas to California, for which Oscar Lewis's *Here Lived the Californians* (Toronto: Clarke, Irwin, N. D.) offers brief historic sketches of significant homes.

Acknowledgments

My thanks go, first of all, to the museum and house curators and their dedicated allies, the officers of supervising committees and agencies, for their generous assistance. For scholarly guidance I am especially indebted to Helen Duprey Bullock, the National Trust for Historic Preservation; Henry M. Judd, the National Park Service; and Charles E. Peterson, F.A.I.A., Philadelphia.

PHOTOGRAPHIC CREDITS

Claude B. Aniol, pages 234–35 (all photos)

Antiques Magazine, page 220 (bottom), photo William H. Shupe; page 245 photo Moulin Studios

Argro Photo and Postcard Co., Art Grossmann, photographer, pages 208, 209

Douglas Armsden, pages 42 (bottom), 43 (bottom), 46 (top), 47, 50 (all photos)

Charles Baptie, pages 148 (bottom), 149

Bettman Archive, pages 34 (top), 58 (top), 80 (top right), 140

Lee Blaisdell, page 244 (bottom)

Mathew Brady, page 157 (bottom)

Andrew Bunn, page 173

Mrs. LeRoy Campbell, Curator, Morris-Jumel Mansion, page 93 (top)

Samuel Chamberlain, pages 22 (bottom), 35 (bottom), 168 (bottom)

Columbia Dispatch Photo by Bob Wheaton, pages 220 (top), 221 (top)

Culver Pictures, pages 26 (top left), 31 (top), 79, 84 (top), 96–97, 197, 200 (top), 230

James R. Dunlop, page 156 (top and bottom)

Essex Institute, page 39

Fairbanks Family, Inc., page 23 (bottom)

Mrs. John Whelchel Finger, President Washington Headquarters Association, Daughters of the American Revolution, page 93 (bottom)

E. C. Forsyth, page 172

Frick Art Reference Library, page 80 (top left)

Louis H. Frohman, pages 9 (top); 27; 58 (bottom); 67 (top); 92; 93 (center); Courtesy Yale University Art Gallery, Mabel Brady Gravan Collection; 148 (top), Courtesy The Board of Regents, Gunston Hall; 164

Index